Points *Life*

VPG Publications
C/O Fred Lanosa, Author
11742 Sunrise View Lane
Wellington, Florida, 33449
www.fredlanosa.com

Ordering Information:

Quantity sales and special discounts are available on quantity purchases by corporations, associations, and others. For details, contact the publisher at the address above.

Printed in the United States of America
Manuscript Development and Editing, Danielle Fetherson

Points *Life*

Not Your Grandma's TIMESHARE

FRED LANOSA

DEDICATION

To my beloved sister, Maria Elena (Lanosa) Barilla. A loving wife, mother, daughter, sister, aunt, grandmother, and teacher. She was all that and much more. She touched the lives of the countless children whom she mentored and taught throughout her 40-year teaching career. Her message was clear: "Strive towards excellence." She insisted on your best work and accepted no less. Her career and life emulated that. She was scholastically excellent at everything and a tough act to follow. As her brother, I can attest to that fact. She also loved the Lord from an early age, introducing our whole family to God's love and faithfulness many years ago. There was no greater gift she left behind than that. Though her life was cut short, she lived out her goals. I dedicate this book in her honor because she never got to live out her retirement, having lost her battle to cancer in 2017. Her spirit lives on and with us always. I miss my sis.

IN THEIR OWN WORDS

I receive countless testimonial letters and thank-you cards from guests who have visited our resort and met with me personally to learn more about the points lifestyle. Here's what they said afterward in their own words.

"Incredible! Knowledgeable and
explained things clearly."
MICHELLE D. *Guest/Points-Owner*

"He won our heart ... If not for him, we
would not have bought at all!"
ALLAN E. *Guest/Points-Owner*

"Fred offered us the most appropriate options
based on our current situation."
WILLIAM M. *Guest/Points-Owner*

"He answered ALL our questions from
a variety of scenarios."
JEFFREY W. *Guest/Points-Owner*

"Superb ... Helpful!"
SUZANNE P. *Guest/Points-Owner*

"Fred was very knowledgeable, was able to explain the program and its benefits to us and wasn't pushy when we decided it wasn't for us."
SEAN B. *Guest/Non-Owner*

"Fred was terrific. He loves explaining the product and he was glad to see I had purchased multiple times in the past. We are believers."
ALLAN M. *Guest/Points-Owner*

"Frederick was friendly, knowledgeable, and did not use high-pressure tactics. I especially appreciated the last part. When it was decided it would not fit our schedules, he accepted that ... he's a real professional."
ROBERT G. *Guest/Non-Owner*

"He was personable and warm. Loved his approach."
STELLA B. *Guest/Points-Owner*

"Fred asked good questions, listened well, tailored his presentation to our specific moment-in-time situation and did not exert any sales pressure. We bought."
DONALD M. *Guest/Points-Owner*

"Fred was very attentive to my concerns and motivations. He's knowledgeable and was able to customize his presentation according to my needs and desires."
ALICIA H. *Guest/Points-Owner*

"Personable ... Professional ... Knowledgeable!"
NICOLE B. *Guest/Points-Owner*

"Very knowledgeable and provided great insightful information."
EDWARD M. *Guest/Points-Owner*

"Straightforward, understood my situation, demonstrated integrity."
JAMES Q. *Guest/Points-Owner*

CONTENTS

INTRODUCTION

My wife was getting madder by the minute. A guy had approached us with some offer for a complimentary $50 dinner certificate to the restaurant we were walking into. I decided to play along even though we were hungry and had obviously been targeted. My wife was not happy and was getting irritated.

"So, why would you give us $50 for dinner certificate?" I asked. The solicitor repeated his offer while pointing to an old apartment building in the distance with three "open house" flags prominently attached to it. To get the gift certificate, we had to stop by that building for a short presentation. It looked sketchy, so I asked him a few questions while my wife grew more impatient with me for playing along and not just blowing the guy off. "Number one, do I have to buy anything? Because I don't have any money. Number two, is this legal? After all, this is *New Jersey*," I said sarcastically with a snicker.

My questions took him aback. He responded, "Yeah, it's legal."

He reassured me that I didn't have to buy anything. I still didn't trust his offer to give me $50 for dinner certificate with no strings attached, so I probed deeper. Finally, the man told me the catch: "I want you to sit through a 90-minute presentation."

My wife and I were newlyweds on our very first family vacation. We had budgeted our fun money to $27 per day plus food money to last four full days. Our funds were so tight, I had calculated the gas we would need to get home. If all went according to plan, we would probably run out of gas just as we got home and literally roll into our driveway. Bottom line—we were lucky to be there.

At that time, there was no gambling in Atlantic City. It was all about the five-foot waves, the saltwater taffy, Mr. Peanut man, the boardwalk, and my childhood memories of the Jersey shore. I had always loved it and I was hoping my wife would, too.

The year was 1977, and that was the introduction to my first timeshare presentation. I hesitantly took the $50 dinner certificate coupon before we headed toward the old building for the presentation. That simple act marked my first fight with my wife. She was hungry and irritated, and just wanted to eat. I wanted the $50.

The bribe worked.

We walked into the old apartment building, which looked ready for demolition. A local developer had bought the building and was renovating it. We joined the bullpen full of people who had also taken the same bribe from the boardwalk, and it was obvious we were at some sales presentation. At the front of this room was a screen for a slideshow and a table with information packets about this new timeshare project. A well-dressed, articulate gentleman welcomed everyone and started his presentation moments after we arrived.

He went into the history of Atlantic City and described how gambling would turn it into the next Las Vegas but with an ocean! I was getting excited, and so was everyone else. He further explained his company's credentials leading to their newest project—timeshare. I must admit, the entire crowd was sitting on the edge of their seats. It was time for the kill. As he wrapped up his opening, the speaker qualified us by asking pointed questions that required participation. God, I hated that part, but I must admit, I was intrigued by the whole concept and what it would be like to own this stuff.

Presenter: "How many people are staying at the Sand Dollar Hotel down the street?"

A bunch of people raised their hands.

Presenter: "You guys are paying $89 a night. How many people here are staying at the Sandpiper Resort?"

Another bunch of people raised theirs.

Presenter: "You're paying $69 a night. How many people are staying at the Starfish?"

He was right on point, as the rest of the attendees raised their hands.

Presenter: "The rest of you are paying $99 a night. Folks, follow me and get ready to see where you could stay next year."

He led us through two doors on the main level to a totally remodeled two-bedroom villa apartment complete with a full kitchen and a living room with a TV and a stereo. It came with a sleeper sofa so we could bring guests, and someone had decorated the whole place to the nines. The *WOW* factor hit me like a ton of bricks!

It was the most beautiful place I had ever seen—it impressed everyone!

Now, you have to understand where I'm coming from. I grew up in a little blue-collar town in Connecticut where we lived very modestly. I had never seen custom drapes and matching floral centerpieces that coordinated with custom carpets. Our furniture back home was made of Formica and stainless steel. Basic and functional would describe it best. This professionally decorated villa blew me away, to say it mildly.

My wife, well, she loved the place but said exactly what I was thinking: "What are we doing here? We can't afford this." To us, the room looked like the Taj Mahal. I immediately went into withdrawal, knowing full well that we were out of our league. My wife was right; there was no way we could afford this.

The presenter gave us all a few moments to take in the view, then broke the silence and lit up the room with a simple question: "How would you like to stay here next year for $39 a night?"

I couldn't believe my ears. Did he say $39? I immediately raised both hands and both my legs too. Yes, I almost fell over! *That* was a price I could afford.

To buy in, all we needed was a $50 deposit, which was replaced with that $50 dinner certificate. It was clever, and it worked. It also made complete sense. More importantly—I *wanted* it. The package we bought was for a 13-year term. It was the cheapest deal they offered, and we later celebrated using the $50 dinner certificate.

I was so enamored with our timeshare that it actually launched my timeshare sales career shortly thereafter. Over the next 13 years, we made memories that still resonate today. It was a great decision for us, but at first, we were unsure about it. Most people are unsure about timeshare when they first hear about it; this book is for all those people who are reluctant like we once were.

Concept To Culture

Timeshare has become a powerful currency-based system. The book title "PointsLife," by definition, defines how a simple vacation concept evolved into a lifestyle, a culture, a new breed of traveler, and a brand for people who love to travel, vacation, and explore the world on points as opposed to cash or credit.

Thirty-plus years in the real estate and timeshare industry has taught me that what most people believe or perceive about vacation ownership is inaccurate.

Most people attend a timeshare presentation because of the gift incentive, not because they want to buy. I'll admit the old, traditional timeshare product has baggage. Some of it is true, and some of it is the venting of disgruntled owners who were misinformed or who dealt with less-than-professional industry salespeople.

It's a fact that Grandmother's old timeshare week was more restrictive and confined to one home resort. This limited weeks-owners to a certain time of the year, a specific resort location, and a certain size vacation villa that, over time, became burdensome to use. So, I get where these opinions came from.

Today, vacation ownership has evolved into a highly efficient currency-based travel system called "points." This book places the reader into the ownership position of points and provides a firsthand look at why consumers buy into the points system reluctantly at first and then buy more points again and again.

The book is jam-packed with solid information, insider secrets, advice, and tips on whether you should own today's *new and improved* vacation ownership system or stay on the *pay-as-you-go* system. Hopefully, you'll gain new insights, allowing you to establish an informed opinion and perspective on one of the leisure industry's most controversial topics. Vacation ownership today isn't for everyone, but it offers tremendous ongoing value to those people who have different travel tastes, a wide variety of budgets, and the desire to create long-lasting memories.

This book is not about your traditional timeshare weeks or explaining how traditional timeshare weeks work. However, you will learn why the vacation timeshare industry had to evolve from buying one-week intervals into a points-based vacation currency system. Points have become the answer to vacation ownership without restrictions.

It's no mystery that old-school "timeshare" has earned a questionable long-standing reputation of low value, high-pressure tactics, and unwanted maintenance fees.

Without requiring you to sit down with a salesperson and make a buying decision within 90 minutes, this book opens the doors to the timeshare industry today, so you can be free to explore the vacation ownership opportunity on your own terms. Consider this book your personal tour guide into an evolved timeshare industry with a focus on how flexibility, variety, and affordability have broken down all barriers over the traditional timeshare weeks. Vacation ownership today has become more of a lifestyle. To take time to vacation, travel, and create memories while experiencing as much of this beautiful world as possible is to live a PointsLife.

I will be forthright in saying that I really hope you will live a PointsLife for yourself. I know what it's doing for thousands of owners who had no intention of ever buying any kind of vacation ownership from the get-go. I'm even throwing in a bonus chapter and some free tools to help you figure out whether this opportunity is right for you.

How to read this book

If you're in a hurry, the key chapters I recommend you read are chapters six and seven. Chapter three offers a bonus and the bonus chapter so you can learn how a PointsLife differs from your grandmother's timeshare of old. You can also learn how vacation owners can get free trips, as well as how to be an owner without paying excessive annual maintenance fees like Grandma did.

But even if you're in a hurry, I encourage you to come back to read the rest of the story to get the full benefit of this insiders' tour.

The pages ahead show you how the timeshare industry is built for deal lovers (chapter one) and has evolved to have fewer restrictions, fewer fees, and less hassle than your grandma's timeshare (chapter two).

You'll dare to dream about taking those world-class trips and what your vacation experiences could be like owning points (chapter three). Inside a PointsLife world, you'll learn to get all the perks of today's pay-as-you-go travel website deals but without the stress, limited customer service, and cash outlays using hard-earned after-tax income to pay for it (chapter four).

Next, you'll dig into the numbers behind vacation ownership to see if they make sense for you (chapter five), as well as read stories about real buyers overcoming real-life obstacles to have vacations that are better than they could ever imagine (chapter six). Then you'll get a checklist that lets you buy with confidence if you think the PointsLife is right for you (chapter seven).

With that said, we have a lot to get to and I don't want to waste your time. So, let's jump right in.

CHAPTER 1

Vacation Ownership Is for Deal Lovers

Several years ago, I had the pleasure of meeting an elderly couple we'll call Peg and Henry. They attended a timeshare tour with me after accepting a gift as an incentive. Henry was 86 years old and acted as if he had one foot in the grave while his wife Peg was a fiery 83 years old going on 44 years young. She was a feisty gal.

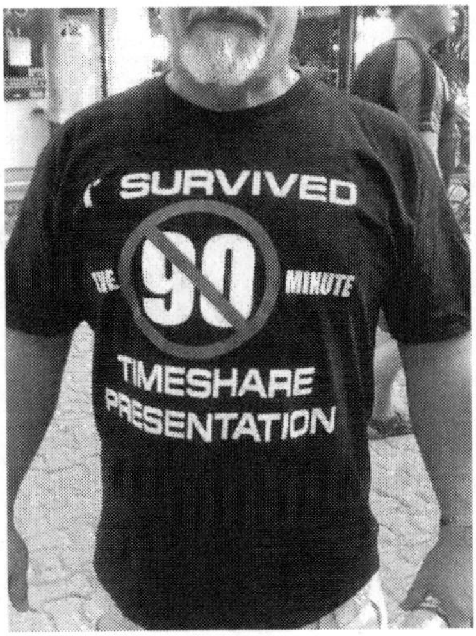

Apparently, they had gone through several timeshare presentations before, so this would be only a matter of routine. Peg was well prepared! Henry was a different story. His personality was that of one of my older, mean, grumpy Italian uncles. His crossed arms and repeated glances at his watch broadcasted his lack of interest from the get-go. My guess was that his wife was the one who had booked the tour, and he resented being required to go.

I introduced myself. They introduced themselves and we kibitzed, hoping to find some common ground. It was awkward – mostly one-word answers and nothing more. Henry was in shutdown mode, closed-minded and most definitely non-conversational. I felt barely tolerated.

Take The Bribe

Peg and Henry aren't the only ones who come to presentations with their minds made up to not buy. If you've ever attended a presentation, that was probably you too. Admit it. I know it because it was me and my wife when we went on that tour in New Jersey.

After being on the professional sales side of the table for more than 5,000 presentations, I've developed a sixth sense for detecting when attendees sit through a 90-minute sales presentation simply to claim the freebie. I call it walking in with a "blood pact" that has been pre-thought-out and predetermined before arrival.

I know about the kick under the table, the squeeze of a hand, or the stern-look signal to the weaker person to not cave in and show interest in the offer. Those signals mean, "Don't forget we agreed that we're not here to buy anything!"

Tricking you into buying something you don't want isn't the goal. If you're willing to attend a 90-minute timeshare sales presentation for a freebie, that really means you're a deal lover like I am. The tradeoff seems worth the battle. Unfortunately, those with true interest have become discouraged about getting the information because the presentation has become more of a sport of endurance. I think the whole thing was heading the wrong way. I wanted to change that by writing this book.

If you're a deal lover who is interested in traveling, vacation ownership can be the best of both worlds: traveling and deals. The point of the presentation is simply to help you understand how every trip you take can be a deal, just like the deal you're willing to wait for on the other side of a 90-minute sales presentation.

So, who really buys this stuff, anyway?

It's for the hard-core traveler who can't take enough trips. The traveler who lives to experience everything life has to offer while they're here on this Earth.

It's for the less-structured traveler. The freestyling, free-spirited, whimsical-souled vacationer who deplores conventional tourist traps.

It's for the non-committal traveler who pays as they go, without committing to anything.

It's for the stuck-in-neutral traveler who says "someday" but never seems to go anywhere.

It's for the frugal-minded traveler who wants to see the world on a dime.

It's for the high rollers who want either red-carpet treatment and the best of the best or nothing at all.

Finally, it's for the "myth-minded" people who would never, ever consider owning a timeshare because of what they have heard, perceived, or believed to be true without firsthand knowledge.

Why the shady public image?

Well, you might ask why timeshare has such a bad rep if it's such a great deal. That's a good question. I don't claim to be an expert in perception, and I haven't made any scientific inquiries into this. However, I think the shady image comes from unregulated past practices to drum up business, which have caused complaints and led to people getting ripped off. I believe there is a combination of things contributing to a "buyer beware" mentality: (1) government-imposed limitations on how the industry advertises and operates regarding educating our buying public and (2) misrepresentation, back in the very early days of timeshare and Florida property sales, by unscrupulous developers, telemarketers, call centers, and intrusive marketing organizations selling beachfront properties in the middle of Kansas. Street solicitors were out there looking to hook unsuspecting vacationers from other markets. That practice screams "caveat emptor," a.k.a., let the buyer beware.

Our American government regulates how all real estate is bought and sold. That's why lawyers and title companies are usually involved when you buy or sell a property. You pay Realtors and other industry professionals a percentage of the transaction to represent your best interests and help you navigate the buying process.

The timeshare industry is a little different. You don't buy timeshare, move in, and live there forever. Instead, you buy into a shared-use ownership arrangement with a bill of ownership rights. You can use the resort property for enjoyment, gift it, share it with someone else, bequeath it to loved ones as part of estate planning, or will it even while you're alive and well. Ownership includes the right to sell it later. However, your ownership does not allow you to redecorate the entire resort to your personal tastes or to sell an entire villa at your resort to pay off your personal debts.

This is a slightly different approach to ownership that can loosely be compared to another government-regulated activity—owning stocks. When you own stock in Amazon, you can gift the stock to someone else, will it to a loved one after you die, or sell it. However, if you think you can sell all of Amazon.com and use the money to pay off your debts or buy something else, you will be sorely disappointed!

Now, with all the money Walmart puts into TV ads about shopping in their stores or online, have you ever seen ads on TV to buy Walmart stock? Have you ever heard a radio ad or seen an online ad to buy stock in Google or Netflix? No. That's because it's illegal.

The ins and outs of the stock or timeshare buying process are more difficult to explain in a 30-second ad than the reasons why you should buy a new brand of vitamin or a new laptop. It takes about 90 minutes for a trained professional to explain the details of a timeshare industry offer and to answer your questions thoroughly.

So, in the absence of the ability to sell through ads that tell you about us, we offer something of instant value, like incentives to get your attention and attract traveling deal lovers to sit down with representatives like myself.

The downside is that, like any industry, we have professionals who are pushy and turn people off. We have owners with buyers' remorse who publish their unfortunate experiences online for everyone to see for all eternity. We have a resale secondary market of unlicensed resellers and would-be brokerages that advertise and try to market resale timeshare weeks and vacation club points without explaining how buying at the discounted prices can limit access to everything you would usually get when buying from the original developer.

The notion of "saving money" on prices with a resale over a brand-new points package or timeshare week from developers is the big claim that resellers are making today. And it's true that you can save money off the price paid. However, the end price you pay doesn't always justify the means, and vacation ownership is a *means* to an end. The end is *the vacations*. If your vacation opportunities are limited, reduced, or even omitted at certain places buying a resale, what's the point? (No pun intended.)

People buy into vacation ownership for many reasons. The two biggest are variety and flexibility. The price is only what you pay for it. Your reasons to buy determine the value. Just keep in mind that resellers typically want to get rid of their timeshare for personal reasons. Their motivation is usually financial, circumstantial changes in health, a death, their children don't want it, or just plain old non-use.

As a professional, I can assure you that all these questions to *get out* were covered before they purchased to *get in*. And the original owners paid the market price to get ALL the benefits, not just a few or less. Also, the developers highlight their level of quality, service, and ongoing support, while none of those things matter to a reseller. Plus, they can't guarantee that ongoing support to a second-generation buyer once they're out of the picture.

Basically, you could be on your own. Even if the original owner is guaranteeing that they received ALL benefits when they bought it, many developers will outline and redefine what happens "after" a resale to protect themselves. Just ask to see the declarations that outline that area. If the reseller can't show you the declarations, walk away!

Keep in mind that when we research and Google timeshare or vacation points, the millions of people who love it and purchase more rarely promote their happiness. They simply use the product and enjoy the experiences. They refer other family members who purchase their own points. They create family memories, see the world at the best rates, and validate the reasons why they bought, year after year.

Relative to the size and scope of that very satisfied and happy vacation ownership market (which contains millions of people), the small minority who complain, write bad reviews on websites, and promote their negative experiences are disgruntled people who lament the fact that they couldn't get reservations on a timely basis. Yet they don't mention that they waited until the last minute to book, did not use it, or experienced a change in circumstances, causing financial hardships that prevented them from taking vacations at all. This negative notoriety casts a shadow over the value we bring to the millions of owners who love what we offer. Therefore, I hope that this book about my experiences will help you move past that dark cloud long enough to open-mindedly consider what we're about.

Now let's look at what it means to join the "silent majority" of happy owners. Millions have turned their ordinary lifestyles into ones of adventure and fun. Many are using their ownerships wisely and enjoying enriched lives—a PointsLife.

How Do Points Work?

Points are purchased once! They are permanent and last a lifetime. Points typically come with a deed of ownership, just like your home does. They can be willed to your children or whoever you want because they become part of your assets and estate. Your annual user benefits never end. Year after year, the same number of points you originally purchased is "re-deposited" into your membership account, and their purchase power increases because of inflation. (The number of points required to visit our favorite locations rarely changes and remains constant.) In a nutshell, the points I'm referring to are inflation-proof currency! It's a very special replenishing bank account, allocated for travel. I call It FUN MONEY or LIFESTYLE MONEY.

The resources available to points owners are more than the actual points themselves.

Throughout the book, I often cite examples typical to the industry. To be more specific, I refer to the organization with which I'm directly affiliated (Marriott Vacation Club). MVC offers four consumer tools, making it simple and easy for members to use the system:

1. Your Member Travel Portal (website): A proprietary website with thousands of pre-packaged vacation options in a menu-driven format. Imagine having the equivalent and resource value of one SUPER SITE that combines the similarity and savings of Hotels.com, Expedia, Travelocity, Cruise.com, Get-a-ways.com, VRBO.com, and Airbnb.com all wrapped into one convenient website? I mention those seven popular portals to paint a solid picture of the magnitude of your membership website and its resourcefulness. You have access to thousands of prepackaged vacations and options. The website makes booking a trip easy and fast. Every resort, hotel room, cruise, tour, vacation house, and getaway destination has its own micro-website, so you can

do your own research and make your own selections at the click of a button.

2. Your Support Staff: Our organization—Marriott Vacation Club—has a support staff approaching 500 full-time advisors on call LIVE, ready to serve. Our members simply pick up the phone and tell them "where and when" they want to go as well as "how big" a villa or accommodations they want. We take it from there using their points (not a credit card) to book their trip. It's that simple.

3. Your Online Points Account: This is an account we set up for every member. It's easy to access from anywhere, at any time, using your own password. It's a secured place where your points can be stored for use, then redeposited automatically year after year.

4. Your Owners Kit: This contains all the hard-copy materials about membership privileges you need. Things like resorts directories, membership CDs, collateral materials, and the like are all right there in one package for people (like me) who enjoy good old-fashioned printed materials. Everything is available online too.

The results are a combination of old-school travel agency service and today's online shopping convenience and nothing but deals galore. Now add the residual power of renewed and reloaded traveling currency (points), all packaged together to create a new standard and lifestyle in travel, lodging, and lifetime value that I call "PointsLife" Vacation Ownership.

Bottom line, points are easy to understand and use, and they recycle every year. You get the same number every year unless you decide to add more. The reservation process is no different from what we do now. We either book our own trips online or call a travel agent, so there are no learning curves.

Our memberships include the assignment of your own personal customer rep or concierge, so members don't have to micro-manage their own vacation accounts or make their own reservations. All you do is pick up the phone to get questions answered, get opinions, and find out how many points it takes to go.

Just like homeowners are responsible for the annual cost of property taxes, insurance, utilities, lawn care, and other common maintenance fees, vacation owners are responsible for their own pro-rata share of annual maintenance fees. However, vacation owners—like homeowners—view those maintenance fees as minor compared to the alternative of renting, in which you still pay for the benefit of living somewhere (in the case of homeowners) or going on a trip (in the case of vacation owners).

The Value

I am asked all the time to put a dollar value on point purchase power. Because value has a subjective personal meaning, I can give you an estimate I find to be accurate if the owner spends their points in an efficient way. Also, what one person sees as valuable, another may not. An example would be a beach lover who prefers to lie on a sun-drenched, sandy beach as ocean waves and crystal blue waters complete a picture of paradise. Another person may hate the sun and get bored lying on a beach, so the values are dramatically opposite. I've said it before, and I'll repeat it. The *cost* of points is the price one pays for them. The *value* is in how you spend them...and that's something you must decide for yourself.

For those needing a dollar amount, points from our

organization optimize at about 2:1. An example would be that 2,500 points in our club are worth about $5,000 in US dollars spent or purchase power in the real world. The variable is always in how well the owner takes full advantage of their membership perks and privileges, which is not equal across the board.

Owners who are on top of their membership privileges, services, and purchase power WIN BIG! If more complacent owners forget about their points, wait until the last minute to book trips, target high-demand times like Easter, holiday weeks, spring break, and President's week, and fail to use the support that's available to them, they are not optimizing their ownership. This may lead to a negative mention or post on a consumer advocate website, which is unfair to the points system.

It's like anything else. There are average, better, and great products, services, accountants, lawyers, tradesman, teachers, administrators, and the like. The same holds true for vacation ownership and its owner-members. There are average members, there are better-at-booking members, and then there are max-out members who leverage every possible benefit available to them. More power to those who are engaged and maxed out year after year!

POINT...CLICK...GO

Bookings. Support. Confirmations.

I've been asked to explain some real examples of trips one might go on using their points and the process for making reservations.

The process is simple: Tell us where you want to go, when you want to go, and what size villa or accommodations you need.

That's it!

Deciding where to go is the fun and exciting part. The anticipation of going away, even more than once, depends on how many points you own. Members simply pick up the phone and call their trip advisor. "Hey, I have some questions about my points, and I'd like to book my next trip. I want to book a trip to Hawaii for January 7th-14th and I need a two-bedroom unit." That vacation request is looked up on your behalf and fulfilled (in our case) with a 95% confirmation success rate, meaning first call, first choice right there on the spot. Yes, you heard me right. Most of the time on your first call! They'll just go into your account, confirm the availability, and book it, giving you confirmation right over the phone. It's very convenient, fast, and easy.

Although nothing is 100% perfect, our points and reservation system is as close to perfect as one can get, in my opinion. Our points system draws inventory from several inventory pools set aside from the public. In addition, discounted vacation trips become available through sudden changes like last-minute cancelations, sudden sicknesses, work demands, and unforeseen life events that happen all the time. Access to room and villa inventory from behind the scenes is derived from all inventory pools, making member availability using points a non-issue because it comes with the assurances of a 95% fulfillment/confirmation rate. This is a statistic that is regularly audited and reported to our members. Our overall owner satisfaction is over 97%, which is driven by fulfillment success! In plain English, you pretty much get your reservation requests using points!

Allow me to dig a little deeper into several examples of points trips so you can see for yourself how much variety in vacation choices points offer. Keep in mind that this is for our Vacation Club for illustration purposes only. Most other developers have their own vacation packages and I advise you to research them for yourself as a comparison. The following numbers are intended to give you an idea of what is possible. Remember the value of points vs. dollars as described earlier. As of this writing, the following are actual trips using points.

EXAMPLE 1: The Big Apple Calling, New York—1,000-point trip*

Imagine spending three or four days in the Big Apple for Valentine's Day to enjoy the pulse and heartbeat of one of America's most vibrant cities for only 1,000 points.

**1,000 points are equivalent to approximately $167 per night your cost in USD.*

EXAMPLE 2: Cruises—from 3,500 points for 2 people*

Maybe you'd like to make it a very special birthday by taking a seven-day Caribbean or Alaskan cruise aboard one of the world's finest cruise ship lines and watch sunsets from an outside cabin.

**3,500 points/couple is equivalent to approximately $250 per night for two people, including meals in an outside cabin.*

EXAMPLE 3: European Land & Sea—from 12,000 points* for 2 people

It's time! Treat yourself and your loved ones to a 14-day European adventure for 12,000 points* per couple. The trip includes destinations like Rome, Florence, and Tuscany, and you'll stay at top-rated European hotels in the heart of all the culture. If that's not enough, you'll then board a luxury ship for an additional seven-day Mediterranean cruise to the picturesque Greek Isles (a.k.a., Santorini coastline). We're talking a real dream vacation here!

**12,000 points/couple is equivalent to approximately $428 per night for 2 people with meals.*

EXAMPLE 4: The Green Shades of Ireland—9,000 points* per couple

Forget the cologne for Dad or the typical bouquet for Mom. Make this Father's Day or Mother's Day special with a 9,000-points-per couple 10-day Irish adventure. You can join an Irish family for a traditional lunch at their farmhouse, spend two nights at the country's most famous castles, kiss the Blarney Stone, dine in Ireland's oldest pub in Dublin, and more.

**9,000 points/couple is equivalent to approximately $450 per night in USD, with meals.*

EXAMPLE 5: 7-Day Costa Rican Adventure—from 8,000 points*

You can go on a honeymoon or anniversary trip with a seven-day Costa Rican adventure to see the forests, waterfalls, volcanoes, and coastlines...or go zip-lining, lounge on the beach, or take a cooking class while you stay at a world-class resort with meals included.

**8,000 points/couple is equivalent to approximately $571 per night in USD.*

EXAMPLE 6: Riverboat Cruises from 13,000 points* per couple

Immerse yourself in the Old World as you sail Europe's most iconic rivers and best destinations: Germany, Holland, Switzerland, France, Italy, Hungary, China, Spain, Portugal, Egypt. Witness Budapest, one of Eastern Europe's most treasured cities, and explore charming villages on a Danube River cruise.

Explore canal-laced Amsterdam and glide to German castles on a Rhine River cruise. Traverse the vineyard-lined Moselle and Main Rivers to quaint Western European towns. In France, savor specialty cuisine and fine wines along Normandy's Seine and Provence's Rhône River. Or behold the splendor of the Elbe, one of Central Europe's most unspoiled rivers. Now you can enjoy them year after year from the Mississippi to Europe... all on points!

**13,000 points/couple is equivalent to approximately $6,500 for 2 people in USD.*

EXAMPLE 7: Vacation Homes—from 7,000 points for the week*

It's no mystery that renting vacation houses has become popular. Now you can rent thousands of incredible houses from two to eight bedrooms, from cottages to castles located on the best beaches, golf courses, ski slopes, and mountains worldwide. Yes...all on points.

**7,000 points for up to 12 people is equivalent to approximately $500 per night in USD*

EXAMPLE 8: Hawaii-Oceanfront 2-Bedroom Villa, 7-Nights Resort—from 4,000 points*

The most popular, beautiful, and luxurious resorts throughout the Hawaiian Islands now honor vacation club points.

Whether you are dreaming of Maui, Oahu, Kauai, or even the Big Island, you'll have plenty to choose from. Today's points resorts offer studios or one-, two-, or three-bedroom luxury villas that sleep up to 12 guests. It's the absolute cheapest yet best way to go.

**4,000 points for a two-bedroom villa with a kitchen that sleeps your whole family, even up to eight people, is equivalent to approximately $285 per night in USD.*

*Price per point varies with each developer, cruise line, hotel, and house, and can change over time.

The Point Of Points

Time is life's greatest commodity, and we all get the same 24 hours in a day. How we spend our time is a matter of choice. Making your life a PointsLife means instilling balance and adventure through vacation ownership. Balance is the wholesome key to a healthy, happy lifestyle. Countless books have been written about balance, but few apply it. Vacation ownership is like having a personal alarm clock that wakes you up and forces you to take a vacation.

Points are a part of the solution when it comes to fun and relaxation. They are so powerful that they force you to do what you may otherwise procrastinate on or put off until another time. That's a good thing! As a professional in this industry, I have a unique perspective on the choices people make. My advice is simple. Remember, we go around only once.

Now that you have a quick overview of what points are and why deal lovers are attracted to them, let's look at how and why timeshare weeks are evolving into more of a lifestyle, a movement, a new-breed culture of wholesome living we call a PointsLife.

CHAPTER 2

Not Your Grandmother's Timeshare

Anyone who has purchased vacation ownership within the last several years can attest to how much it has improved. Today's vacation ownership, in a nutshell, has evolved from the need to buy a specific week at a specific resort restricted to a specific time into a highly efficient currency-based system that's totally user-friendly. Vacation ownership today is jam-packed with options and a variety of choices over a lifetime. In addition, if it's deeded vacation ownership (an important question to ask if you're considering buying), it can be willed or passed down generationally. Consider it a family asset that can not only be passed on to loved ones but also enjoyed year after year in place of the vacation dollars you're spending anyway. Today's consumer is highly informed when it comes to travel because of the internet. Consumers seek value, convenience, and real deals...and they want them now!

Over the years, we've learned that today's consumers want:

» Fewer restrictions with more choices
» Lowers fees with more value for the money
» Less of a hassle to use with first-choice destinations
» Confirmations—not substitutes—for their first-choice destination

I'll tell you what the industry has done to deliver on each of those points, and you can decide how well we've met each standard.

Fewer Restrictions...More Choices

Old-school timeshare weeks are all about owning access to a one-, two-, or three-bedroom villa, in a specific building, in a specific resort, for a specific week of the year. You also have the choice of trading it through a third-party vacation brokerage house like RCI (Resorts, Condominiums International) or II (Interval International), two of the larger exchange companies with which many timeshare developers have affiliated themselves over the years. The "trade" is a two-party transaction. Timeshare "weeks" owners must deposit their week to create banked currency for themselves; they give up "use" of their week that year so that they can withdraw the week of someone else who has done the same thing. Thus, a fair trade is possible. Be advised that there are more variables in trading weeks than just using points. Securing your top requested destination and dates requires all the stars to line up. This makes planning unpredictable and more difficult. It can be a roll of the dice.

With points, you own vacation currency that refills into your membership account each year and that you can use like money. Book any room size, room view, resort location, and time you want by calling directly, just like you would with a credit card. Instead of having your ownership tied to a specific resort location, unit size, and season, which determines the value of what you can spend, your ownership is connected directly to a developer (the source), which archives hundreds or even thousands of destinations, lodges, or vacation homes within its network, in addition to connecting to the same exchange companies that traditional timeshare week owners use. You get both!

This shift means fewer restrictions and more choices in terms of when or how you vacation. Let's take a closer look at how this impacts your experience as an owner.

With Grandmother's timeshare, I remember her telling me about the resort at which she used to vacation each year: how they added some timeshare villas there and that she had an opportunity to buy in early while prices were cheaper. She and Grandpa were invited back to learn about this new way to vacation at her favorite resort. The 90-minute tour, still used today, is the most commonly used method for buying timeshare weeks. It typically starts with an invitation to buy an inexpensive vacation package at a great value that includes a mandatory 90-minute presentation tour of the resort. Your purchase would be for a specific week at that resort, which in effect becomes your home resort. Your final purchase would include a specific unit number, size, and season (time of year). This means that year after year, you would vacation at that same resort, during the same week of the year, and in that same villa. This would become your second home for vacations.

Traditional timeshare weeks also offer "priority" whereby you can select the season or time of year best suited to your vacation time. They price seasons according to demand and popularity.

Depending on the resort or trading system, these seasons are labeled either Red, White, or Blue, or either Platinum, Gold, or Silver. Red and Platinum seasons have the highest demand and popularity, while Blue or Silver seasons have the lowest demand and popularity. As you can imagine, the higher the demand and popularity for the week, the higher the price to buy it. Also, the higher the demand and popularity of the location during that week—like a Red week in Florida, Aruba, or St. Thomas—the higher the price to buy into it.

If the only time of year you can travel is the summer when the kids are out of school or near Christmas when they're out again for winter break, you're probably competing for the higher demand seasons at the higher prices for your home resort.

The off-season or shoulder times are less busy and offer bargains at the same resorts. If you don't care about prime seasons but simply want the ability to go, that might work for you and your pocketbook.

Just be advised that choosing a discounted week with lower demand will affect your trading currency power because your week is less desirable to other owners looking for a trade. In a traditional timeshare, "trading" involves tapping into the resort's exchange company network of resorts to find an owner at another resort who wants to trade their week at their home resort for your week at your home resort. So, if you own the first week of August at Myrtle Beach, but this year you want to travel to Texas during the second week of August, you'll use the exchange company to complete that trade with the member-owner of a timeshare week in Texas who wants to trade in their week for something else using the same network—in this case, the second week of August who is also willing to trade.

Many traditional timeshare week owners bought into the old timeshare system for the ability to trade when they want. However, trades happen only when there is a match between what you have to offer and what other people want to give up. Oh, and because you buy into a certain place, a one-, two-, or three-bedroom villa, that can affect whether you get the trade you want.

The PointsLife Vacationer

The notion of being confined to the same resort year after year is gone. Points owners want the excitement of knowing that they can do whatever they want wherever they want. It's about freedom, flexibility, and variety. After all, sometimes vacationing is about *not having to do anything*.

A PointsLife vacationer's journey begins with an invitation to an inexpensive discovery vacation package to the location of your choice within the developer's network. Your trip includes accommodations in a studio, one-bedroom, or two-bedroom villa for three to five days plus a 90-minute presentation tour of the resort that offers an example of the quality you can expect from the developer. You'll also see a sample of the variety of locations the developer has to offer. This can include beach properties, mountain properties, spa resorts, and secluded getaways. You'll also learn about the properties to which you have access through the developer's exchange company partnership. Exchange companies often open thousands of additional domestic and international travel options.

More than 140 countries take part in timeshare networks. From the most popular destinations to the most private and exclusive hideaways, you have more to choose from than ever before. Today—because of the Internet—it's as easy as point... click...go!

USE POINTS, NOT CASH

Enjoying a PointsLife-style over pay-as-you-go means using

points—not cash—as your currency to purchase a greater variety of travel opportunities. Each developer has different elements in their offer, but as an example, I'll describe what Marriott offers to its PointsLife-style vacationers.

1. Resorts. The world's best resorts are a big part of countless vacation ownership networks. Marriott's resorts are on the best beaches, ski slopes, mountain ranges, and golf courses in the world. Remember the full kitchens, pools, whitewater rafting, and other amenities I mentioned before? They're all included when you stay at their resorts.

2. Cruises. You can use points to buy incredible cruise packages, which include free upgrades, on just about every major cruise line—including the popular riverboat cruises at up to 50% off.

3. Tours. You could also use points to go on thousands of unique travel tours within the United States or abroad. For example, if you want to go to the Midwest to visit any of the national parks, there are plenty of option using points for that. People who want to visit Italy, Spain, Israel, the Scandinavian countries, Australia, New Zealand, Iceland, Africa, Peru, or anything international can use their points to book those "once-in-a-lifetime trips," too. Keep in mind that there are hundreds of prepackaged tours for two people, including meals and even a guide if necessary. The value and vast selections are off the chart.

4. Vacation Homes. Move over, VRBO and Airbnb. You can now use points to rent vacation homes all over the world. Thousands of privately-owned homes can be accessed through a points ownership program, and the choices are amazing, ranging from cottages to castles. These vacation homes are selected for, and located in, the more popular destinations, like beaches, ski slopes, mountain ranges, and golf courses. The days of taking the family to a mountain ski cabin or a four- or five-bedroom oceanfront house are back again at discounted prices using points. Did you ever consider celebrating your 10-year anniversary or perhaps your upcoming 20th, 25th, or 50th anniversary in a romantic Italian villa in Tuscany, Italy? Now it's possible and affordable with points. We've even seen members use their points to rent large, luxurious mansion-size homes for wedding receptions and special events. These homes can range from two to 20 bedrooms in anything from a quaint stone cottage to a large castle. Points owners gain access to those houses at drastically discounted prices...repeatedly.

5. Hotels. The organization for which I work as of the time of this writing happens to be the largest hotel company in the world. There are more than 1.2 million rooms, more than 30 unique world-renowned hotel brands, and, collectively, more than 6,000 hotel locations and growing. That's just in the hotel division alone, so when you put the sum of all that together, your choices are endless. They're all available at the click of a mouse, or they're a phone call away at substantial discounts using your points program.

TRAVEL ON IMPULSE

Are you a last-minute traveler? If so, points offer a real solution. A PointsLife-style is perfect for the business owner or professional with an unpredictable schedule. Maybe your career is demanding and very time-restrictive such that you can't plan something 12 months out. Instead, you have to go at a moment's notice. Or you aren't disciplined enough or don't have a desire to pre-plan, and you love the notion of getting out of Dodge for a few days on a whim. Points fit into that lifestyle like a hand in a glove. Owning points is well suited in these cases.

So, to summarize what we've learned thus far, a PointsLife-style offers much to be experienced in travel, be it resorts, cruises, tours, vacation houses, weekenders, or hotels! My advice is to KNOW what you are saying NO to. Getting the unbiased facts is the key and it's why I wrote this book. Consumers who have toured for the right reasons—to learn and be educated—are often elated that they did!

Accommodations used to be the only thing in the old timeshare days. A PointsLife-style offers accommodation, amenities, airline tickets, event tickets, value, convenience, and equity all in one. Amenities can include private natural swimming pools, fully appointed fitness centers, pro-designed 18-hole golf courses, luxurious health spas, outdoor hot tubs, exciting excursions like hiking, biking, and horseback trails, or even white-water rafting, to name just a few.

Imagine the ability to tap into a network of theme-based resort properties like Disney or the national parks in the Midwest.

If being active with lots to do is more your thing, plenty of destinations are health- and nutrition-centric. Sports-minded vacationers can enjoy resorts that feature tennis, golf, skiing, and equestrian activities...even zip lining!

The PointsLife-style is a FUN-nomenon: a modern culture that includes fewer restrictions and more choices than traditional timeshare week ownership.

Fewer Fees...More Value

Our modern values with respect to variety and efficiency could not be better demonstrated than through the evolutionary coffee by-the-cup movement. This was a game-changer for coffee lovers and it's why the Keurig coffee machine has become so popular. It took me a long time to succumb and buy one of these "per-cup" coffee makers. I told my wife that I refused to pay between 60 and 90 cents for a cup of coffee at home when I could just buy it by the pound for five to seven dollars and make pots full of coffee whenever I wanted. I could make a lot more coffee for less money.

Then she pointed out that we make full pots daily but throw away four or five cups in the pot because we never drink the coffee after it sits for 60 minutes or so. It dawned on me that she was right.

The no-waste factor coupled with the convenience of one cup at a time made it better and more efficient. The coffee is always fresh, I get dozens of choices of gourmet coffee flavors, and I ultimately enjoy it on demand. **That is better!** The funny part is, if someone tried to lure me into a coffee presentation to convince me that the Keurig coffee method of brewing was better, I would resist it and enter the presentation convinced that it wasn't for me. My premeditated pact "not-to-buy" upon arrival would be justified based on what I'd heard, plus I'd have to consider the initial purchase price of the machine plus the ongoing costs of each of those individual coffee modules at 60 to 90 cents each.

Hmmm, sounds familiar.

Aha…I finally got it.

Let's take a closer look at your grandmother's timeshare and upgrading to points as a vacationer to see how this Keurig by-the-cup phenomenon applies when we compare fees and value.

FEWER OPTIONS…MORE RESTRICTIVE

By now we understand that when your grandmother bought her timeshare week way back when, things were different. The industry was new and uncertain. Timeshare was the alternative to renting and people were curious. Timeshare ownership involved a two- to three-hour presentation during which you were offered the opportunity to buy a specific week and possible upgrades at premium prices, such as a high-demand week like Easter, spring break, July 4th, or Christmas. In addition, you could pick a bigger, more spacious unit with better views at higher prices. Then, of course, there was the option to buy lower priced, less-desirable weeks of the year or smaller units, like a studio with a parking lot view, or both. Prices were arranged according to season, size, and views. Your grandmother may or may not have received a deed of ownership with her purchase, but if she got the deed, she could will it to anyone she wanted, or sell it. The drawback was that whatever she chose at that time…was permanent.

She bought into that one location as her home resort, and as an added value she could trade her week(s) in a "my-resort-week for your-resort-week" scenario. The resort's trading power is the key to any chance of enjoying successful trading experiences later and is always subject to availability. So, if she chose her home resort wisely and had a desirable week to offer, she had a decent shot at finding a trade. If others weren't as interested in her home resort or week as she was, her added value option of trading was hindered, and she may have been stuck with a dud.

Limited.

If Grandma wanted to take her grandkids on a road trip across the country and stay at different hotels along the way instead of staying in a resort, she couldn't use her traditional timeshare week at all. Cruises, vacation houses, trip packages, and any non-resort vacation experiences were not options.

Inefficient.

Timeshare week vacations are broken into seven-day increments. If Grandma wants to take a 10-day vacation this year, she'll be forced to buy another full week, or seven days' worth of vacation time. That will result in four unused days every year. If Grandma prefers short getaway trips, the seven-day timeshare week is still a problem. Either way, the inefficiency of weeks ownership could make for wasted time.

Here's another situation in which weeks ownership is restrictive. Let's say Grandma's newest grandbaby is due to be born during her annual timeshare week (it happens) and she wants to be there to see her little one. If she can't find a trade match in time, she'll run the risk of wasting her week altogether or being forced to go when she can't. What if she wanted to gift her week to the new parents so they could get caught up on sleep after three months of life with a newborn in the house? Dad would have to be able to take time off work when Grandma's week arrived, or Grandma would have to successfully switch her week dates to a time when they could go. She would run a risk that this week would be unavailable.

Keep in mind that her annual maintenance fees are paid on all seven days, while she may be using only three days (wasting four days) or, worse yet, not be able to go at all (wasting all seven days). This is often referred to as “use it or lose it.” If she trades for a different resort, in most cases she pays a separate fee for that too. Occasionally there are those special celebration years when she chooses to get a bigger unit or multiple units so she can bring all the grandkids. However, she may be out of luck unless she can find that trade match.

Originally, she purchased her timeshare week based on travel being cheaper “by the pot full,” a full pot vs. by the cup (each individual trip). When you look at how our trip preferences and needs change over time, it’s “variety and efficiency” that come up short or as being more wasteful. Grandma’s week has less value and has become diluted over time. That lowered value combined with the requirement to pay fees, like it or not, does not make that old, traditional timeshare week look like a sizzling hot deal.

Fees.

Keep in mind that Grandma paid a fee anytime she traded to another week or another resort. In addition to that fee, she paid her annual maintenance fee for her home resort, whether or not she used her full seven days.

During the early stages of the timeshare industry, timeshare weeks were designed for old-school vacationers who went to the same place during the same week each year. It was a deal when you consider buying a vacation home as an alternative. However, for today's traveler who values efficiency and variety for minimal fees, it comes up short.

A Better Solution

In comparison to timeshare weeks, points are easier to work with. It's pure currency. Continuing with the Marriott example from above, you're buying the currency that's accepted at all the resorts, cruises, tours, vacation homes, getaways, and hotels within the developer's network(s). That's total flexibility. It also comes with a deed of ownership, so you have the choice to will, rent, or sell a portion or all of your points.

In old-school timeshare, owners' options were much more restricted. Let's take timeshare's most popular feature: trading or exchanging to another resort. An owner's trading power using their week(s) was based on which resort they bought into—more specifically, which week, which season, which size, and in which home resort. All these choices played key roles in one's trading success. Points ownership eliminates all these variables. Thus, they become a non-issue and you end up with real freedom.

Declare Your Independence

Points don't restrict you to one place or time. In a nutshell, it's the vacation ownership alternative with no restrictions. It's a universal currency for travelers worldwide. You can spend it in any denomination or amount you want. If you impulsively decide to go away for just three days for a little getaway, you peel off enough points for three days' worth and go. The balance remains in your account to use another time—a whole new perspective on vacation ownership. If you want a clearer picture, consider that new and improved version used by millions in another culture—the coffee lover and the Keurig coffee machine. That change took time. It proved to be a preferred method. It directly affected an entire industry.

Points mirror the Keurig coffee phenomenon. Today's PointsLife-style is a culture; a Declaration of Independence for vacation ownership. Points are to vacation ownership what Keurig is to a new-breed coffee-drinking generation—an on-demand product packaged with value and variety. Always fresh...many flavors...zero waste and you spend it as you need it! Comparatively speaking, with the entrance of the Keurig coffeemaker, today's coffee drinkers now prefer freshly brewed coffee on demand, by the cup, by the flavor, creating a KeurigLife—the better solution.

Points became the answer to having variety at the click of a mouse. Using our points, you can book thousands of available hotels while en route to your cross-country road trip or go on quality cruises from four-day to 21-day world-class European adventures. Enjoy family reunions in fully appointed three- to eight-bedroom vacation houses or rent multiple condominium villas, townhomes, and suites in luxurious resorts if you choose to relax in a total resort setting. If that's not enough, you can always go on international travel and guided tours loaded with optional local excursions, making choices simple and easy. Again, all with points.

Because points ownership members own in all the resorts within their developer's resort network, you no longer pay trading fees to the trading companies. The eliminates one of the biggest gripes about timeshare...junk fees!

Points represent everything we love about vacation ownership and eliminate most of the restrictions and costs that discouraged purchasing.

EFFICIENT

You can use your points to book trips that are as short or as long as you'd like. If you want the 10-day Irish adventure trip this year for 9,000 points per couple, book it. Are you more in the mood for city lights in the Big Apple? Just call, book, and go on a 3-day New York getaway for 1,000 points per couple.

If your annual membership account doesn't have enough points for the trip you want, borrow the extra points you need to fulfill your travel plans from the following year. You then return to your normal point balance.

If you want to upgrade to a higher number of points permanently, that too comes with more privileges. So, in addition to the added vacation time, you can aspire to VIP status levels and become a higher priority traveler, which comes with greater discounts and more benefits.

The upgrade option is always there for you as a member. Many members choose to upgrade their ownerships by returning to the resort for an update tour. Many members call their sales executives directly to touch base, ask questions, and possibly upgrade through a mail-away purchase or request a return update trip that serves as an inexpensive way to grab a few extra days of vacation while at the resort and to learn what's new.

Many returning vacationers are invited to events during their vacation stays or to a seminar or private tour that allows them to better understand all the new changes and brings them up to date. Our members are the lifeline to a successful vacation ownership organization. We welcome return visits and in most cases, we're there on site to counsel valued members and even their guests. Upgrading is easy and affordable and typically comes with additional owner incentives.

If you have points left over after your trip, you can roll them over to the next year, rent them out to someone else, or gift them to a family friend. Nothing goes unused, and you don't have to wait for another owner somewhere else to agree to trade anything with you.

PointsLife means first-choice confirmations.

No one enjoys getting the runaround when trying to book their reservations. No one likes a bait and switch or being underwhelmed when they finally arrive at their long-awaited vacation destination to find out the resort looks nothing like the pictures.

For most of us, our vacation(s) arrive only a few times per year. So, getting the destination you really want, the accommodation(s) you want, and the time of year you want means having a great vacation experience right from the beginning. The anticipation of going, the planning, and the personal service are what make vacation ownership so much better at every level. To get that kind of caring, assurance, and attention to detail not once but every time, customer service in the timeshare industry had to step up their game. Today's vacation ownership has done just that.

Let's look at the difference between the ownership experience of a traditional timeshare weeks owner and the experience of a PointsLife-style vacation owner.

WEEKS ARE WEAK

So long as Grandma wants to stay or return to her home resort during the week she bought, she should be fine with that reservation. After all, she owns the deed to that week's time slot. However, if she wants to trade her week to another resort location, the process becomes more involved. It becomes a "wait and hope" system

She needs to:

- SWITCH: Call in her official request for that desired resort location. *Ex: Put her request in early enough for unforeseen things.*
- SIZE: Hope her requested villa size (one-, two-, or three-bedroom) is available that week. *Ex: She really needs a three-bedroom but there's only a two-bedroom available.*
- CONFIRM: Wait for the exchange company to confirm her request in a timely enough manner so that she can finalize all the other plans. *Ex: She still must coordinate the rest of her trip plans, including other family or friends who must arrange pet boarding, ground transportation, school, mail, job, etc.*
- ALTERNATIVES: Hope she gets the resort she wanted and not alternative suggestions. *Ex: She requested Aruba, but the exchange company came back with a suggested available unit the same week in St. Thomas or Florida.*
- If airline tickets must be purchased, run the risk of buying tickets in advance of the resort confirmation or vice versa.
- Wow! That's a lot of stars that need to line up.

Another consideration is the quality of the timeshare week

Grandma is using as her trade currency. If Grandmother's owned-week is at a more popular resort and a high-demand time, she'll have no problem getting her week scooped up by another vacationer. But that's only 50% of her exchange. The other 50% is getting what Grandma wants for giving up her high-demand week!

Successful exchanges are really a "two-part transaction." Certainly, it won't take long for her week to get absorbed by another vacationer. However, finalizing her trade match may be another story. The flip side is if Grandma owns a low-demand week or resort that doesn't attract much interest, her trade request can be even more difficult or uncertain.

During the process, if she gets desperate to go anywhere, she may not get her first-choice location and will end up settling for a trade to a resort she doesn't want, a time slot during which she'd rather not travel, or a two-bedroom villa when she really wanted a three-bedroom villa.

So, after weeks of waiting for a trade and not getting exactly what she wanted, how happy will Grandma's vacation experience be? Do you think she'll be excited when she talks to "non-owners" about timeshare ownership?

ZERO LEARNING CURVE

After years of evolving due to consumer demands for a better way, today's ownership programs have transformed so that they no longer include traditional weeks whereby you bought the right to use your week(s) from 10 to 99 years into an individually owned "deeded asset" with all the rights of passage from one generation to the next forever to the end of time. A giant step for mankind.

Those restrictive old timeshare weeks that trade through

"hassle-to-use" third-party exchange companies have been replaced by direct-connect, no middle man, bigger, better, and easier-to-book worldwide networks. Simply pick up the phone to talk to a real, live person trained to help you get the trip you want or use your developer's website to book online. Instead of paying with a credit card (cash), you pay for it with your points.

That means a zero learning curve. Points ownership was modeled from the exact same process for its members and it has never been easier to book the trip you want. The vacation network with which I work has one of the highest success rates in reservation confirmations in the industry—a whopping 95%. In plain English, if you lined up 100 families, 95 of them will get their first choice of destinations. This is a far cry from timeshare weeks that operate using a request-wait-hope system.

Because vacation ownership is totally turnkey, today's PointsLife vacationer can enjoy all the best parts of ownership while leaving all the headaches of ownership behind. A successful management program is the key to your future enjoyment. As owners, you want the resorts and their villas to look clean, fresh, and new when you arrive or return.

You want the staff to be friendly, courteous, and helpful. You want live support (not recordings) when you need it. You want things to be properly maintained and replaced when needed so that neglect doesn't create special assessment fees later. Ultimately, you want accountability on the part of your developer to maintain the integrity and continued quality of what you purchased. Isn't that right? Of course it is, and we all want that quality built into an asset we are considering buying.

All those assurances in points ownership are included and ongoing. The good news is that you get all this at a minimal fee:

a maintenance fee. These fees usually include management, real estate taxes, insurance, utilities, staffing, refurbishing, and long-term deferred maintenance. Again, in my case, our organization completely refurbishes each villa with new furniture and furnishings every 60 months! It's all included. Imagine if someone came into your home every 60 months to do a total remodel for a minimal annual fee.

In other words, this is a hassle-free, hands-off ownership opportunity at its best. Remember, deeded points are real estate ownership. Nothing that can be "owned" typically comes without the need for maintenance along the way. Your car, whether leased or owned, and your home, whether rented or owned, has maintenance costs. In a PointsLife world, total maintenance and management are shared amongst thousands of owners, reducing a member's cost to pennies. You're getting more value, services, and support for your money.

MAINTENANCE-FREE

Many major-brand vacation clubs are helping their owners pay little or no maintenance fees annually through referral incentive programs. When you join the PointsLife User Group on Facebook, you can learn more about maintenance-free options as a special gift from me to you.

It's a simple-to-use system that can strategically eliminate your timeshare maintenance fee and membership dues without the need to sell, rent, or lock off your timeshares. To learn more, go to www.Maintenance-Free.com.

Key Takeaways

Gone are the days when vacation ownership meant you were restricted to a specific location, a specific week, in a specific unit...forever.

Here are the top 10 reasons to consider owning points:

1. It's easy to understand.
2. It's easy to choose.
3. It's easy to use
4. You can bank unused points.
5. You can borrow next year's points or upgrade by buying more.
6. You can share points with family and friends.
7. You can will points to loved ones, charities, or anyone you choose.
8. You can gift points to others without going yourself.
9. You can exchange to other resorts easily with points.
10. You can sell points.

In a PointsLife world, vacation ownership means traveling on your own terms, wherever, whenever, with whatever size accommodations you want. Whether you break it up into a series of quick getaways, go away seven days, or travel for a month, it's all up to you.

Not your grandmother's timeshare.

CHAPTER 3

The Big Question

Imagine that you are a contestant on a game show and are going for the grand prize. It's between you and one other person. The pressure is on. Focus is key. You are down to the very last thing to win it all! You must answer the BIG Winning Question within 60 seconds. Your answer must sway the judges and be *Convincing, Enthusiastic, and Imaginative*!

Here are the final two rules:

1. *Money is no object.*
2. *The Best Answer becomes the winner's grand prize.*

Q: Describe that Once-in-a-Lifetime, All-Expenses Paid, Fantasy Dream Vacation in the next 60 seconds.

The clock starts NOW!

Hmmm....how did you do? Do you think you would have won? Were you able to whisk yourself away to that tropical paradise? Was the allure of Europe calling your name? Could you describe the feeling of going to Australia? Did you dream BIG enough, or are you like many people today who never give those dreams much thought because they're caught up in the routines of life?

It's hard to not like the idea of taking a big trip like this, but it's also hard to know whether you'd really take such a big dream trip if that isn't something you usually do. This is also part of the reason why it's hard for some people to see themselves living the PointsLife dream.

Vacationers who can take these kinds of trips as often as they want are typically already traveling and enjoying life. Taking vacations is not an issue for them at all. Their issue shifted to learning about a new way to experience more of those trips at much better rates and savings. PointsLife travelers know why points are a better currency and outperform hard-earned money, cash, or credit. It's proven.

On the other hand, if going away is harder for you by nature, points provide that extra nudge you need. If that sounds like you, points are most definitely your solution. You get the needed nudge and savings. The key is three-fold: recognize, decide, and take action to make a better life...a PointsLife!

Go back to the BIG question and start thinking, describing, and—better yet—planning more and more dream vacations for yourself. The points will provide the means.

What Is A Points Vacation Planner?

I created a custom points vacation planner because it gives new owners a chance to see how points vacation ownership enables them to easily plan great vacations in minutes. The vacation planner is a simple spreadsheet calendar template you can use to plan vacations, including the best times to go, what size villa or accommodations you need, and the number of points necessary to make it happen. The planner takes only a few minutes to use and saves hours of time, prevents missed deadline dates, and eliminates the need to settle for what's available instead of first choices. Once you put together a planner, you've created a plan to enjoy future trips while taking all the guesswork out of points use. In addition, points vacation owners will get the most out of their ownership and it's a lot of fun!

If I can get you to think a little bit ahead of time, the planner becomes very resourceful, and dream trips are more likely to become reality.

FREEBONUS:DownloadaFREEPointsVacationPlannerKit with instructions by going to www.PointsVacationPlanner.com.

Start with One Vacation Where...When...How Long?

Sometimes the use of points can seem confusing, but nothing could be further from the truth. It's quite easy. It all starts by planning just one vacation per year for now to keep it simple. To determine the number of points it takes to book different types of trips, refer to the downloadable points planner bonus at www.PointsVacationPlanner.com. All you really need to know is where, when, and what size of accommodations. Points are configured by the day or week, meaning you know exactly how many points it takes to stay per night. That information can be found in resort directories provided by your membership, or online at your membership travel portal. If you understand how to plan for one vacation per year using points, adding more trips is a matter of buying additional points as needed. Don't make this hard; simply think about what you love to do, whether a vacation that's warm, beachy, and tropical; skiing; golfing; hiking trails in the mountains; or even one of each. Whatever you dream of doing, now is the time to write it down and plan it out.

Here are the four steps:

1. Buy some points.

2. Book your trip.
3. Roll over any unused balances for the next trip.
4. Repeat forever.

Imagine planning unlimited vacations, year after year, on points (not cash). When you own points, you are much more likely to go! I call it the "nudge." For example, laying on a beach in Aruba would be one choice. If golfing is your thing, would a five-day trip to Hilton Head, South Carolina be attractive? I think you get the idea.

The objectives of owning points are numerous. Variety... quality...savings...it just works! Points are a lifestyle boost—thus, the name of this book, "PointsLife." It's a new kind of vacationer. If you need some inspiration, here are some tips to jump-start your creative brainstorming for what you can do on your vacations over the next five years. In chapters four and five, we'll talk about how you'll pay for it. For now, we're setting travel goals.

Single with No Children?

Wow! The world is at your fingertips.

Again, are you the type of person who enjoys a warm, beachy, tropical island?

Are you all about cultural trips (like Europe)?

Do you gravitate toward the hot spots, nightclubs, music, and city or urban vacations?

Is a Caribbean, Alaskan, or Mediterranean cruise more your thing?

If adventure is your style, why not whitewater raft down the Colorado River on a four-day excursion with friends?

Are you a skier? A tennis player? A golfer?

Maybe it's time to tap into your passions and make them the

themes of your future vacations.

If You're Married or Have Children, Here Are Some Things to Consider...

Think about whether you have children or plan to have children in the next five years. If so, there's a good chance that the next several years will include child-centric vacations. That means Disney World and other theme-based locations, as well as national parks and important locations we may want our children to see, like the White House and the Smithsonian in Washington, D.C.

These points vacations would most likely be scheduled during the summertime. That's when the children will be out of school.

Age Matters Here...A well-thought-out vacation planner plots where you would like to go relative to the kids' ages. For example, let's say your children are four and eleven. Now let's go out five years. That means next year they'll be five and twelve, then six and thirteen, then seven and fourteen, and so on.

Future Point-Spend...Forecasting your point consumption in advance is a great benefit of ownership. It not only gives you the ability to think about essential trips you would love to take but also enables you to strategically use your points to get there. I call it optimizing your points. Learn all about "optimizing your points" by going to www.PointsVacationPlanner.com and downloading a free vacation planner.

Imagine knowing you can take those "must-do" trips without worrying about whether you'll have enough money at that time. Whoa! Let me explain. Points are like a vacation annuity. That means you buy them "once" and each year thereafter, that same amount of points gets re-deposited into your account...

forever! The best part is, you never have to buy them again; you just keep enjoying them year after year! The comfort of knowing you can plan future family vacations in relation to your children's (or grandchildren's) ages is priceless. For example, going to Disney is more enjoyable when the children are old enough to appreciate the animation and splendor of the Magic Kingdom. Points enable parents to plan those trips with a certainty of going and to experience them with the children while they're still at home. Remember, you get only about 17 summers with them before they don't think you're cool enough to hang out with.

Those kinds of future events make owning points and a well-thought-out points planner invaluable.

Tips for Travelers Old Enough to Qualify for Social Security

Time isn't less important when you're older; it's more important because you have less of it. So, what are some places you want to revisit or explore for the first time?

A planner puts into perspective the use of this thing in a very important way. You could get yield not only out of the points but out of the cash they represent—and most importantly, the time.

Vacation Planner Next Steps

Have your list of annual destinations and the length of your trip? Okay.

Later, you can add the guys' trip or girls' trip you're overdue for, the trip to the annual family reunion, the graduation for which you'll need to travel, and any trips you'd love to gift to others for their graduation, honeymoon, anniversary, or just because. However, for now, your list should focus on one trip per year until you get the hang of using the planner.

If you were sitting down with me right now, I'd walk you through the number of points you'd need to take the trips you want over the next five years. However, because I'm not with you and I don't know what you wrote, I'll spend the next couple of chapters letting you listen in on me walking others through points vacations and the process of comparing the power of using points over pay-as-you-go, seeing how the numbers add up.

Key Takeaways

Collect your free bonus: Download a free vacation planner kit with instructions from the author by going to www.fredlanosa.com.

Use it to help yourself plan all the trips you'd like to take over the next five years. Keep it handy as you go through chapters four and five and make a practical comparison of what those same travel plans look like with and without points vacation ownership.

CHAPTER 4

Pay-As-You-Go vs. Pay with Points

I can't see what you wrote on your five-year vacation planner, but I'm willing to bet that if you put a realistic dollar amount next to each trip, say $4,000-$5,000 *(FYI: seven-night vacations today average approximately $4,000)*, you would be shocked when you looked back over time and added it up. That's when most first-time buyers get their epiphany or aha moment! Financial logic kicks in as you reflect on your vacation dollars being spent in any way over time or "waste-shock" value. During the same five-year period in the illustration below, it would cost you approximately $25,000 of hard-earned, taxable income. That means, depending on your tax bracket, you would have to earn approximately $5,000 gross income to net $4,000 after taxes to buy your $4,000 vacation! You would repeat that year after year for five years! What if you were asked to pre-pay for a five-vacation package for $25,000. Would you? Probably not but that's exactly what you're doing! Comparatively speaking, most people are elated to learn that it takes approximately 2,000 points to pay for a quality, one- or two-bedroom villa with full kitchens. Two thousand points are valued at approximately $4,000 in purchase power. Hmmm...the wheels start turning. The investment is the same $25,000, and most people who normally would get "sticker shock" soon realize they were paying for it anyway. The truth of the matter is, the exact same amount of money over the same five-year period is being spent! The difference is that points buy vacations forever, for life, not for only five years. They are willable in perpetuity. Points are protected by a deed of ownership. Points price-freeze future inflation costs for accommodations. Points require no sales tax and can be gifted to your kids, transferred into other members; accounts, rolled over for future use, etc.—which is better for you and your family if you are going to continue taking vacations with or without points. Check out the illustration below to see for yourself.

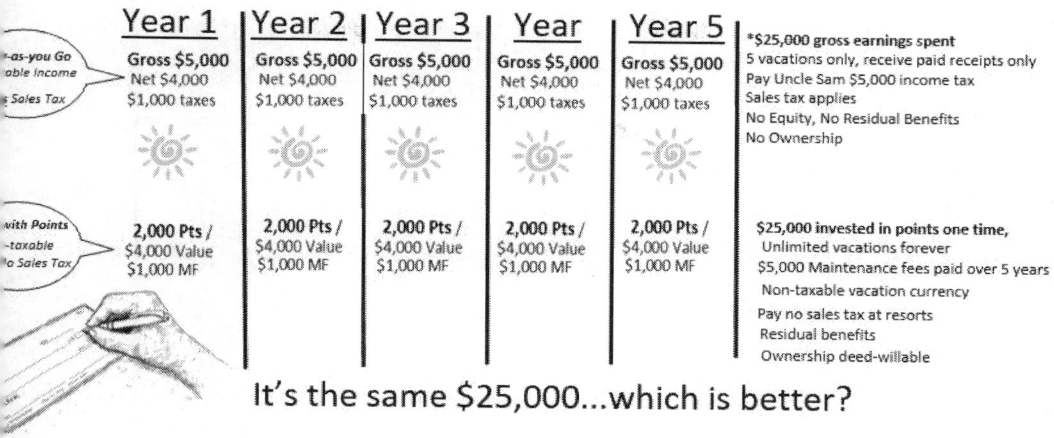
Year 1
Gross $5,000
Net $4,000
$1,000 taxes
2,000 Pts /
$4,000 Value
$1,000 MF
Year 2
Gross $5,000
Net $4,000
$1,000 taxes
2,000 Pts /
$4,000 Value
$1,000 MF
Year 3
Gross $5,000
Net $4,000
$1,000 taxes
2,000 Pts /
$4,000 Value
$1,000 MF
Year
Gross $5,000
Net $4,000
$1,000 taxes
2,000 Pts /
$4,000 Value
$1,000 MF
Year 5
Gross $5,000
Net $4,000
$1,000 taxes
2,000 Pts /
$4,000 Value
$1,000 MF
*$25,000 gross earnings spent
5 vacations only, receive paid receipts only
Pay Uncle Sam $5,000 income tax
Sales tax applies
No Equity, No Residual Benefits
No Ownership
$25,000 invested in points one time,
Unlimited vacations forever
$5,000 Maintenance fees paid over 5 years
Non-taxable vacation currency
Pay no sales tax at resorts
Residual benefits
Ownership deed-willable

It's the same $25,000...which is better?

That's okay, and it's normal. This chapter is all about helping you compare apples to apples by looking at your list of dream trips and comparing the costs of pay-as-you-go using hard-earned money and of owning and using points as your travel currency. By the end of this chapter, you'll clearly see the advantages of points over cash. I'll even tell you how you can take one or more of these trips for free!

Let's eavesdrop on a conversation I had a while ago with a hesitant buyer. I asked where they would go if my company bought them an all-expenses-paid trip.

Hesitant Buyer: "That's easy. We've always wanted to go to Hawaii. We probably would go for two weeks and visit two islands. That would be a dream vacation if we could go for two weeks and island hop."

Fred: "That would be a great trip! What do you think a trip like that might cost?"

Hesitant Buyer: "I don't know. Two glorious weeks in Hawaii island hopping, seeing the sites, with food and airfare—maybe $10,000."

Fred: "Okay, that sounds about right. But let's say you were paying for it out of your pocket. Would you really part with

$10,000 in cash? After all, that's hard-earned money you had to work for."

Hesitant Buyer: "I don't know...when you put it that way, hmmm...not sure. It depends on whether it was a one-time thing. Maybe I would."

Fred: "Up to this point, have you ever done anything like that? Would you really go into your savings account and pull out the $10,000 for one vacation?"

Hesitant Buyer: "I don't know about $10,000. My husband and I are bargains hunters. I'm sure I'd find us a great deal if we looked hard enough. I believe I could find that same two-week Hawaii trip for less than $10,000. I don't see why we'd have to buy *points* when I can find great deals. I bet I can get that trip at 50% off or $5,000 if I really shopped for it."

Fred: "Okay, we're getting somewhere now. So, you're telling me that one reason you may not buy points is that you could most likely find that $10,000 Hawaiian vacation cheaper...say, $5,000 as a great shopper? Is that what I'm hearing?"

Hesitant Buyer: "Yeah."

Fred: "Okay. Let's fast forward. You decide to go to Hawaii, so you shop around and find a deal for $5,000. Would you really take $5,000 out of your checkbook?"

Hesitant Buyer: "Yes, we would!"

Fred: "That's fine but because we're comparing your currency to mine, let me explain what $5,000 really represents. Because you're buying it with income, you must go to work and earn approximately $7,000 to $7,500 gross and pay Uncle Sam income tax on it, to be left with the $5,000 you need to buy the trip. So, let me pose the question again. Would you pay $7,500 gross for that $5,000 trip to Hawaii?"

Hesitant Buyer: "Hmmm...I didn't think of that. No, I don't think we would."

Fred: "Thanks for your honesty, but if the points were sitting in your account waiting to be spent...would you go?"

Hesitant Buyer: "Well, heck yeah, we'd go!"

That is the Point of Points! If you had to choose between your checkbook or a bucket full of vacation points as your method of payment, one would make you go and the other would make you stay! Points make you go. Your checkbook could make you stay. My suggestion is to buy the points once and never again look back or worry about going.

Buying Online Deals Is For Losers

When I hear people talk about the deals they can find online, I ask what makes them so confident they can get better deals online than they can as a points vacation owner. Often, the consumer cites hearsay and third-party water-cooler talk about vacation ownership being more restrictive, an obligation, a system that confines owners to one specific resort or time of year. In other words, most of their objections are to Grandma's timeshare weeks, not points vacation ownership.

At first glance, vacation ownership will appear more expensive when it's stacked up against simply buying one vacation at a time. The norm is to buy vacations one year at a time. Doing it that way is a habit and doesn't reflect those costs. However, the compound effect of that same pay-as-you-go travel system makes the trips more expensive when you add them up. You must look at both methods side by side to clearly see how the value and buying power of points clearly wins over pay-as-you-go. It's been called a no-brainer.

It really puts the value into perspective when you compare your actual spending habits into total vacation costs over five, 10, or 20 years. I call these *anyway dollars* because it's the money you'd spend *anyway* whether or not you own points. I can then take the same money and convert it into a viable vacation points package that matches the person's interests and budget. It's a conversion. It's re-purposing the same money you will spend and putting those dollars to work for you by investing them into a points package that will continually fund annual vacations forever, not one at a time.

The bottom line is, with vacation points over real money, you'll get higher-quality vacations that are value-packed, not once but every time! We love getting a great deal. It's in us. To save money or become better stewards of it is important because of what we do to earn it. Simply put, we get up, get ready, and go to work, and before we get to spend the money, we pay taxes on it! Ouch! So, real money is painful to part with. On the other hand, vacation ownership is a special means or currency set aside as your fun money. If you consider the number of other things that put a stranglehold on your checkbook, you may never go on vacations.

You May Be a Vacation Owner If...

I think Jeff Foxworthy—the stand-up comedian and TV personality—said it best in his famous self-identifying "redneck" skit in which he recites all kinds of scenarios that stereotype the redneck lifestyle. He is famous for his "You Might be a Redneck" jokes and other redneck humor. For those of you don't know, "redneck" is *historically a derogatory slang term to refer to poor white Southern farmers in the United States.*

Jeff's quotes:

> *"If you've ever made change in the offering plate, you might be a redneck."*
>
> *"You may be a redneck if...your lifetime goal is to own a firework stand."*
>
> *"If you own a home with wheels on it and several cars without wheels, you just might be a redneck."*

I find it funny when you apply that self-identifier to vacationers. This separates people into three groups that can be identified as follows:

» You may be a <u>Retail Traveler</u> if...
» You may be a <u>Retail-on-Sale Traveler</u> if...
» You may be a <u>Vacation Owner</u> if...

Let's examine each one to see where you might fit. This is in jest but if the shoe fits...

You may be a straight Retail Traveler if...paying full room rates is normal, expected, and never given a second thought.

You may be a straight Retail Traveler if...staying in discounted hotels without amenities and full services is absurd to you at every level.

You may be a straight Retail Traveler if...you frequent the hotel's health spa, shop the hotel's expensive boutique clothing stores, and ask for late checkout even if it means paying for another full day.

It's common for this type of consumer to skip the coupons and discount clubs and opt to pay $600...$700...$1,000 per night if need be. This isn't to say that all retail travelers won't take advantage of a good deal when they can, but a deal isn't the most important thing. The straight Retail Traveler is most likely not our ideal demographic. Saving isn't their hot button!

Now, the Retail-on-Sale Traveler is a whole other story. They would most likely be attracted to the benefits of vacation ownership because they love the notion of saving money and getting bargains. They pride themselves on their clever, money-saving expertise. In that regard...

You may be a Retail-on-sale Traveler if...you are a relentless bargain hunter.

You may be a Retail-on-sale Traveler if ...you refuse to pay full retail and will buy only if it's on sale.

You may be a Retail-on-sale Traveler if...you're willing to go on a cruise and take an inside cabin with no window, on the same deck as the staff, for the best cabin rates....

You may be a Retail-on-sale Traveler if...you're excited that the parking-lot-view room just became available so that you can save on hotel room rates.

You may be a Retail-on-sale Traveler if...the off-site parking lot, only a 15-minute walk down the street, is fine for you because it means saving a $10 valet parking charge.

You may be a Retail-on-sale Traveler if...you have attended multiple timeshare presentations just for the gift, bribe, or cheap trips.

I'm exaggerating the point here, but the truth is that Retail-on-Sale Travelers make great prospects for vacation ownership because the system offers the very best deals all the time without the hassle of having to search for those deals. Great value is built into every vacation package.

On the flip side, there are millions of vacation owners today who were once Retail-on-Sale consumers. Today, vacation ownership has become a culture that you may welcome into your life. We call it a PointsLife.

You may be a prospective Vacation Owner if...you want the very best accommodations at the cheapest rates.

You may be a prospective Vacation Owner if...you like the idea of bringing the family together for reunions where everyone can get a bedroom.

You may be a prospective Vacation Owner if...freedom of vacation choices excites you, like going to spectacular vacation resorts, luxury hotels, Caribbean and Mediterranean cruises, vacation houses on the beach, international tours, or quick getaway packages.

You may be a prospective Vacation Owner if...passing your ownership rights onto your children is important to you.

You may be a prospective Vacation Owner if...gifting trips to your family—like anniversary trips, Mother's Day or Father's Day weekends, honeymoons, Valentine's Day escapes, or special celebration trips—appeals to you.

You may be a prospective Vacation Owner if...every vacation must be an on-sale deal.

With vacation ownership, your points or vacation currency prices freeze all future rates to today's prices. That means accommodation rate increases will no longer apply to you or your family. You don't have to worry about your favorite destination doubling in price down the road. In addition, the number of points required to stay at the resorts will typically remain set forever, which caps future resort inflation once and for all.

If you usually take at least one trip per year, the savings are obvious. However, if you tend to take (or want to take) two or more trips per year, the savings and value are off the chart. Therefore, many points vacation owners buy more points later and add more to their ownerships down the road.

Points Strategies You Can Use to Optimize

You already know that points renew in your membership account each year and can be used to book a variety of trip options with fewer restrictions, fewer fees, and less of a hassle than your grandmother's timeshare. Now you see how using points allows you to leave cash in your savings account while you travel. Our next step is to see how you can strategically use points to hit your travel goals in ways you can't through pay-as-you-go travel methods and websites.

Most people don't know that points owners can roll unused points over into the next year and borrow future points by pulling them into the present year if they need a few extra points to go somewhere. For example, you might plan to visit Florida this year. However, instead of going for a seven-day week, why don't we go for six days and roll the unused points over until next year? Now you have enough points next year to take a cruise.

You may think you can visit a travel website and book a shorter trip, then use the saved money to go on a cruise next year. However, when you own points, the full number of points you bought one time will replenish itself in full, 100% reloaded automatically each year back into your account. Points perform just like a vacation annuity. I call it a 401-V. So, imagine adding the leftover points from this year *to* your newly refilled supply of points from next year, enabling you to go on a more expensive trip at no extra cost. Do you have cash that automatically fills your savings account each year and that you can use to travel?

Perhaps this year—due to an undetermined work schedule—you want the freedom to do a few three-day getaways instead of a full seven-day week. Points are the solution.

Your vacation points planner (go to www.VacationPointsPlanner.com) is the manifestation of what points can buy and do, what they are, and how they'll fit into your lifestyle with total flexibility. The reason that's so important is because you go through life in stages. What you once liked, you may not like anymore. What you do now may change in the future.

I remember the very first time I bought brand-new furniture as a newlywed in my 20s. I bought this god-awful big Paul Bunyan oversized pine furniture. It was the coolest thing you could buy back then. However, today that's the kind of stuff you'd find on the sidewalk on trash day or in an antique shop.

Your taste, and what's important, and things that you'd like to do will evolve and change as you get older, as your children get older, and as you begin seeing options. That's why points and a planner are so resourceful.

The vacation planner is also something visual that you can easily reference and change as you check things off your bucket list if you have one or want one. It takes the guesswork and mystery out of understanding the points system.

Point Yield...Get Two Vacations for the Price of One

I learned this "two-for-one" technique while talking to my experienced points owners. It works so well, I adopted it as a "pro strategy" and teach it to all my first-time buyers and uninformed existing owners. More times than not, existing owners will add points to upgrade their ownership to implement this technique. So here it is.

Everyone deserves at least one vacation each year, but when you use this strategy, your points ownership will get you two trips for the price of one. To illustrate my point (no pun intended), let's say a typical seven-day vacation in a two-bedroom villa at a beautiful beach-front resort destination like Florida, Hilton Head, St. Thomas, or Aruba is 3,000 vacation club points.

When you understand how flexible and powerful points really are, you can get clever with their use to optimize their buying power. For example, if a points owner is willing to vacation six days instead of seven, from Sunday to Friday, that slight adjustment reduces the number of points required by 50%! That means you can purchase a six-day trip with 1,500 points vs. 3,000 for a full week. Now ask yourself this question: Would you be more excited about owning points if you could take two six-day vacations instead of one seven-day vacation in the same year for the same 3,000 points?

This strategy works extremely well because in our system there's an approximately 50% difference in points-to-go between a weekend point rate (Friday and Saturday) and a midweek point rate (Sunday through Thursday).

Now consider this example and the joy of selecting the best ways to use your 3,000 points of ownership. If you have a family with children, you can use the first 1,500 points to take a fantastic six-day family vacation, maybe to Disney, the Grand Canyon, or some outdoorsy, adventurous resort.

The choices are endless. Believe me, as a father of five; your kids would love to choose the vacation places they want to visit. Points ownership makes it affordable and possible every year. The other benefit is that it leaves you with another 1,500 points for a romantic couple's vacation for just Mom and Dad. Yes, up to six days to some tropical beachfront resort without kids or whatever you love to do. In other words, you could take that second six-day vacay for yourself. Or you can optimize the use of your 1,500 points by breaking them down into a couple of weekend getaways for just the two of you. Now, that's being strategic with your points.

Strategic Ways of Finding Free Upgrades Using Points

One of the reasons I love showing points owners how to use a vacation points planner is because it helps them see where and how to spend their points before they go on their vacations. The planner maximizes great use and incredible value in yield. That means zero waste out of their points ownership every year.

Let's revisit the 3,000-points illustration one more time. Say you went on a seven-day vacation that used up 2,000 points. You would have 1,000 points left over in that current year. Most owners would be content with rolling the 1,000 points over to a future year—which is smart if you planned on taking on a trip next year that required additional points. However, you could also opt to fine-tune the current year's trips to enjoy a better experience by asking yourself:

- Do we want to stay longer on the trip(s) we're taking?
- Do we want to get a bigger villa so that we can invite family or friends?

- » Do we want to upgrade our view to oceanfront, as opposed to garden view?
- » Do we want to take an extra weekender this year because we have extra points?
- » Do we want to surprise a loved one with a weekend or getaway trip on us for graduating or for a birthday?

I call this process *fine-tuning*. It's how you can find additional weekend trips, better views, extra bedroom space for guests, and free upgrades. It's usually in the crumbs that fall off the table.

Trust...It's the Most Important Thing

Points are priced individually, and prices vary depending on the brand you decide to join. Points are like e-currency (a Bitcoin for travel) and have purchase power the same way money does. The difference is the brand, the size and scope of the network(s), and the variety that that brand will offer you. In chapter seven, you'll learn more about what to consider when choosing a brand, but for now, note that the difference between brand names and independent developments is typically a matter of choosing the flavor that you like best.

People may buy into a specific timeshare because they frequent a certain location. For example, they may love going to Cape Cod, Massachusetts. Because many of the major brands may not be in Cape Cod, they opt to buy into a small, parochial timeshare. There's nothing wrong with that. The end game is that you're happy.

There are reasons why one brand or location is preferred over others. Having worked with many different resort developers over the years, I have found that you're safer with one of the major brands. The bigger brands certainly got that way for a reason.

However, big doesn't always mean better for you. I want to be clear and fair about that. I don't want to make you feel like you're being sold one brand over the other. When I'm in front of my tour guests, I can learn what they do vacation-wise and then advise them accordingly. Similarly, I want you to arrive at your own decisions based on what I know and share because it's insightful and resourceful to your situation, lifestyle, and budget.

There are the big brands like Marriott, Hilton, Wyndham, and others, which offer great products and many locations. Then there are the independent developers and less-known brands that sell niche locations. What's important is that major brands offer certain things that smaller brands do not. Plus, when you choose your company, keep in mind that your taste may change over time. What made you buy it at first may not be the reason you decide to keep it later.

As I mentioned before, when I was in my 20s, I went with my wife to buy furniture for our first apartment. Back then, big, bulky, Paul Bunyan-type pine furniture was in style and trendy. That appealed to us. Today, that same furniture would be sitting out front on the sidewalk, waiting for the donation truck to take it away. Bottom line, our taste changes over time. Back then, Paul Bunyan furniture was trendy and there was nothing else I would buy at that time. I will admit that our little studio apartment stuffed with oversized pine-wood furniture was the envy of my friends, and I know I caused a lot of pine furniture packages to be sold...lol!

Sticker Shock...When you compare pay-as-you-go to the price of a vacation ownership package, the value and actual savings become crystal clear. There are times when I will meet a family with no vacation money budgeted, in which case everything looks too expensive. Those cases become more challenging because there is no vacation commitment to begin with. I would have to say that it's those types of people whom vacation ownership helps the most, above and beyond the savings. They need that annual nudge to go away or they won't do anything at all.

One of the biggest hurdles in deciding to buy into a vacation ownership system is seeing the total price of vacations packaged as a one-time purchase, all at once. I call it sticker shock, not because it's too much money but because the consumer isn't accustomed to looking at a lifetime's worth of vacations all at once.

The other challenge with vacation ownership is the maintenance fees associated with it. Most consumers are not accustomed to paying a maintenance fee to go on a vacation. Upon a closer look, the truth is, you do pay a maintenance fee to go on vacation. Nearly 70-80% of room rates are profits and 20-30% go toward maintaining the resort or hotel. The difference is that vacation owners do not pay any more profits and they save that 70%-80% paying only their share to maintain the asset they own with others. Once the initial cost of the vacation ownership package is paid for, owners get to travel on just their maintenance fee, which can equate to about 20-25 cents on the dollar or 75%-80% savings forever!

Anyway Dollars...A great way to break down the purchase price of a points package is to look back in time at what you have been spending as a matter of habit—in other words, the *vacation dollars* you spend anyway, without points or any kind of ownership.

An example of that would be a family or individual who has no problem spending $2,000-$5,000 on a seven-day vacation. In this case, the consumer can reflect on their spending habits by looking back in time—say, five to six years. They can easily see that they could have paid for the vacation ownership package in full already.

Those spending habits could easily justify the purchase of a vacation ownership package because it's no longer a matter of creating a new bill but, rather, of re-purposing money already being spent moving forward.

The financial logic is that they are buying it anyway...just one year at a time, with no residual benefits or deed of ownership that's willable (in most cases) as the prize later.

The economic and long-term advantages of owning far outweigh the costs of pay-as-you-go methods, no matter how smart of a shopper a person believes they are. These days, my life is centered more around educating the consumer and less around selling them. Both existing owners and prospective members appreciate being educated about what points are and how the system works best for them.

The financial gains realized over time become a byproduct of owning and not the only reason to buy. The truth of the matter is, vacation ownership creates a certain lifestyle and an ongoing commitment to fun and relaxation that comes at a price either way.

The Strategic Use of Points...One of the most interesting aspects of owning points is the strategies and fun ways to take full advantage of their flexibility. This is because points are easy to understand as a currency and are easy to use. Just point-click-go or pick up the phone to make a reservation. Now and then, I still come across owners who find that they have either too many points or not enough points left over at the end of the year.

Those are the most fun tours because I get to counsel the owners on becoming more strategic in their planning. It's a lot of fun and productive for both of us. I'll coach them how to optimize their points to get more out of their ownership. I show them how to create a simple vacation planner that stretches out over a five-year period jam-packed with free upgrades like oceanfront views, bigger units, and extra days they missed because they had to be shown how to plan strategically.

It literally takes 10 minutes to show owners the ropes, and they leave thrilled about their purchase. In many cases, they upgrade their ownership by adding points. Points can be pushed ahead and pulled in through borrowing. Because of those features, being strategic is easy. A strategic thinker or person who prides themselves on being a great shopper will love owning points. It means getting more for less...all the time.

Managing and manipulating one's points becomes a game we play and win every time. The use of forethought and strategy means you can step back and fine-tune your trips with additional days, better views, or even multiple units when bringing families together for a reunion.

Suppose you went on a year's worth of vacations on points and had a few left over. Most people don't realize that those leftover points can be rolled into the next year. The points can be added or combined to give you more total points to use the following year. By adding to the annual reload, you may have enough points to take a 14-day trip to Italy or Ireland, or even go island hopping in Hawaii...all pre-paid with points strategically used!

You see, those types of trips require a few more points, and strategic planning is a surefire way to get there using your points, not your money. When you become masterful at using points, vacation ownership opportunities are endless. That's why most of my meetings with people are informative and consultative, showing them creative ways to use their ownership that they didn't think of. They see firsthand the wisdom of adding a few more points—to experience more.

TRAVEL ON IMPULSE

Are You a Planner or Impulsive Traveler? Today's travelers fall into one of two groups—planners and impulsive. Because points owners can take better advantage of their options by planning their vacations earlier than the public, I don't like to give the impression that planning is a prerequisite to owning.

If I'm talking to people who are educators or administrators, planning is important to them and is second nature. I try to emphasize the planning advantages of owning points.

If I sense that people are free-spirited and live life on the edge, or their schedules or businesses are more demanding, points work incredibly well for them too. Points are so powerful as a tool and currency in both scenarios because "last-minute" trips as well as long-range planned trips offer great value.

With points, you can go very impulsively, in as little as a few days out. Or, if you prefer to take full advantage of your planning window and yield, you can book your vacations from 12 to 13 months in advance. It's such an incredible advantage over the general buying public, who typically cannot book a reservation earlier than six or seven months out using cash or a credit card. Vacation points owners, a.k.a. vacation club members, typically get the very best accommodations and the lowest rates...all on points.

The points system I personally represent provides members

with many options not found in other points programs. Should you desire to visit a location with no resorts, you have direct access and the flexibility to tap into hotel chains from more than 30 national brands, covering more than 110 countries. Later, we'll discuss what to consider when buying into a points network. However, rest assured that you'll want to join one with an expansive collection of places, variety, and destinations you can visit no matter how remote they are.

Key Takeaways

The message is clear—points are the new timeshare. Today's vacation ownership has evolved into a more sophisticated system of travel. Therefore, we can't allow old timeshare sales tactics and unscrupulous high-pressure practices undermine the product itself. Today's information is readily available in this book and online.

The ease of researching and obtaining relevant information should pave a new road for open-minded consumers who can now learn for themselves what this new vacation movement is all about. The high-pressure 90-minute sales presentation, a.k.a. resort tour, has evolved along with the product. You will find that today's vacation ownership presentations are more consultative and advisory to convey the new timeshare message...and that is the point of this book.

CHAPTER 5

Point-o-Nomics

Do the numbers make sense? As we toured the grounds of the resort, Peg couldn't help but take in the beauty and relaxed atmosphere as I explained the benefits of our program. I talked about how our members get to create and share these wonderful experiences with their families and friends.

Long story short, we got to the end of our tour and now it came to the money—the bottom line. The vacation ownership package Peg wanted cost about $30,000. When I wrote that price on the whiteboard in my office, Henry experienced immediate sticker shock! He looked over at me, looked back at his wife, and looked back at me a second time in total disbelief. Remember, this is a man who never spent a dime on vacations, so any amount would have sent him into a tailspin, let alone that amount.

Henry: "Peggy, do you realize it's going to cost us about $10,000 a year to go on vacations for the amount of time we'll use this thing?"

She looked at him with fire in her eyes, then looked at me and asked if I would kindly step out of the room so they could talk alone. I had no idea what would come next, but I knew something was brewing and about to boil over.

By all outward appearances, the presentation had opened a can of worms and I lost hope that this would end up good. Nonetheless, I peeked into my office about five minutes later only to find them in a deep conversation. I certainly didn't want to interrupt, so I politely asked if they needed a few more minutes. She signaled me with a hand gesture for another five minutes.

Concrete Financial Examples

Vacation ownership isn't for everybody. Therefore, I won't get offended or upset if you don't run out and buy one after reading this book. The truth of the matter is, you have already taken the first step toward educating yourself simply by reading this book.

Points are the new timeshare, and because of the old timeshare myths, they remain a misunderstood product even though points can add so much quality to one's lifestyle. The information right here is all you really need to take the next step.

Remember Henry, who said he just wanted to be alive in three years? You never know how much the vacation ownership experience can mean to those you love until you think about the lifestyle and value it can bring to you and all those around you. The PointsLife is a higher quality life that's everlasting.

That's a quite different value than the cost of the points themselves. When people ask, "What do points cost?" or "What is the price?", really what they're asking me is, "Will the cost of purchasing it, along with the maintenance fees, really make economic sense?" The answer to that question must be separated. The cost is what you pay for the points one time, while the value will always be how you spend the points. That's year after year...forever. So, let's cover that in this chapter.

Cost is NOT Value

There are basically three kinds of travelers. The first kind is the thrifty type who will be hard pressed to part with $100 per night. Then there's your more quality-conscious traveler who might spend $200 to $300 because if they're staying in a place, they want it to be clean and nice. Then, of course, there's the luxury traveler. That's the status-minded person who will spend $400, $600, or $1,000+ per night because they can. They prefer VIP treatment and all that makes them feel valued while staying there. They want the view, the valet parking, and the best seats at dinner, and they'll spend lots of money for those perks, privileges, and benefits. The question is, what kind of traveler are you? Budget, quality, or luxury?

Knowing your motivations helps you determine how ownership may or may not work for you. It comes down to some good old-fashioned financial logic, a.k.a.: Do the numbers work? If you find yourself thinking that you just don't have the money to be a vacation owner, pause and ask yourself how you are able to afford the trips you have been taking. And remember that the price of your vacation points covers a lifetime of vacations, not one trip for a single year.

Do you consider yourself an avid shopper or the consummate deal-seeker? Well, I was born in New York and raised in Connecticut, so I can relate to the Northeastern mentality and our need for a good deal. As a rule, Northeasterners do not pay retail for anything, let alone vacations. Regardless of the item, if it's not on sale, as a rule, we simply won't buy it.

On the other hand, most people like to get a good deal on any purchase. It's human nature, I suppose. So, if you're savings conscious, I would be very inclined to say that owning vacation points will be a great fit for you. You will feel good not only about the quality vacations you're taking but also the incredibly discounted prices you'll be getting by using your points instead of your cash.

If you've realized that you will go on vacations whether or not you own points, vacationing itself is a part of your life. This means you've decided to vacation or treat yourself to fun, rest, and relaxation at your favorite resort, cruise, beach, or wherever for at least one week out of 52 per year (hopefully more). We all deserve that.

With that being the case, the question isn't "Are you going?" The question shifts to how you pay for it because trips are not free. Up until now, your hard-earned cash paid for your trips one at a time. Now we'll look more into the numbers behind why hundreds of thousands of people prefer to make a one-time purchase into a lifetime of trips using the reusable currency of points.

What is points purchase power?

Owning points creates much more than pre-paid vacations. Points owners cross over from renting to owning a vacation currency asset that can buy them any vacation they want for life.

Stop and think about that.

The asset itself creates an ongoing "vacation income" that is tax-free.

That's right. Each year, points produce enough purchase

power and value to allow you to take vacations that otherwise you'd have to pay for with your income.

Let's say I'm talking with someone who spends about $3,000 a year on vacations. I'll point out that they're using taxable income to go on those vacations.

Here's an example of what I mean. Let's say you decide it's time to get out of Dodge and take a vacation. You go online and visit all the popular travel websites offering discounted vacation packages. Suddenly, you stumble across a stroke of luck: a great resort in Aruba that's screaming *BUY ME!* The dates are right, the resort looks great, and the price is ridiculously cheap. You go for it!

QUESTION: What made you buy?

ANSWER: The deal.

You were deal-hunting, on a mission and looking to buy, and you found something of great value! A beachy, warm, tropical vacation worth $4,000 but on sale for $2,900. Wow! A $1,100 savings!

You buy it using a credit card, which will be paid off later... using what? Your ordinary income. If you forget to pay it off in full when the credit card bill arrives 30 days later, add compounded interest at credit card rates to the cost of the trip.

Now, if you're like most Americans in the 15% tax bracket, you'll also add taxes plus social security payments to the earnings necessary to buy your trip. Figure another 25% on top of what you really need to earn to buy the trip. [2017-http://www.taxpolicycenter.org/model-estimates/baseline-distribution-tax-units-tax-bracket-march-2017/t17-0018-number-tax-units-tax].

Bottom line, you would need to earn approximately $3,744 gross income and pay Uncle Sam his portion, leaving you with

$2,900 net with which to purchase that vacation package...and that's a fact. So, you're still paying $3,744 for a $4,000 trip. Not such a great deal after all. Plus, if you enjoyed the trip and wanted to do it again the next year, you'd have to go to work to earn the same income again with no guaranty that prices on the same trip won't go up. Oh, and if anything is automatically deducted from your pay, like health insurance, retirement, and other employer benefits, you'll need to earn enough to cover that too.

Points are the better currency with which to buy annual vacations because you don't have to continually re-earn them. They replenish themselves each year. Buy them once and you can spend them again, and again, and again while you keep your hard-earned money in the bank. Points enable you to stay in the best places at the cheapest prices.

Value and savings are usually the motivators for true deal-lovers. Vacation ownership is the solution to get both.

How are points purchased?

Most developers package their points in minimum increments depending on how their resort costs are evaluated with respect to their point value. In other words, it's a rates-to-points-to-dollars ratio.

Different resorts have different underwriting that goes with their points. If you were to compare major brands like Marriott, Hilton, and Wyndham, you may find that while they operate similarly, their evaluations may be very different. It just depends on the system you're in and your preference in terms of the locations and brands they offer. Typically, when there is more to offer a member, the points purchase power is higher and the savings can be significant.

Before I make any recommendation as to the number of

points you should buy as a new member, we'll consider your vacation habits. If you have no vacation habits, consider where you would love to go in the future.

Remember when we talked about the trip(s) you would take if you didn't have to pay for them and mapped it out on your vacation planner? This is how that plan connects to the points you buy. Estimate the type and frequency of trips you'll take each year, and determine how many points they cost. That will give you an idea of the number of points that are ideal for you.

What can I expect to pay for vacation club points packages? Prices are easy to calculate once you know the purchase price per point. The formula is the number of points times the price per point.

Just like typical pricing for houses and cars can vary based on the economy, points prices vary among developers and according to what is going on in the market. They usually will go up in value, which is contrary to old-school timeshare weeks, which tend to go down in value, becoming worthless.

Quality branded resorts typically offer starter packages for about five to 10 days' worth of points in the $10,000-$20,000 range. It's a one-time purchase. That one-time purchase provides a lifetime of annual vacation income for that amount of time, tax-free, using inflation-proof currency!

If you generally spend $3,000 per year on your own vacations, you would break even (in value) on a $15,000 points package by your third or fourth vacation. Not bad considering that after your third or fourth vacation, you can continue taking annual vacations forever using the same points over and over!

The frequent traveler who vacations several times per year or who takes extended stays one to three months at a time can purchase big packages at greater discounts upfront, making the value even better. Many of my clients have bought larger packages in lieu of purchasing a second winter or summer home.

Points owners can have the freedom to live in great locations for extended stays, foregoing the big financial outlays necessary to buy a second home. Where, when, and how you spend your points is all about what works for you, but the possibilities are almost limitless.

Sounds expensive, I don't think I can afford it

This is a common feeling once our guests learn how extravagant they can vacation using points.

Now that you understand the power of points and how they compare to spending your taxable income, let me show you how you're already buying points now without knowing it when you budget or save for a trip.

Whatever you are accustomed to spending on vacation each year...whether it be $1,000, $3,000, or $5,000...the principle is the same. If your vacation "anyway," dollars set aside come from taxable income. Here's an example. Let's say you're comfortable spending $3,000 per year on trips. If we divide that amount by 12, you'll see $250 per month as the amount you'd need to save toward the pay-as-you-go trip. And this is after-tax dollars, so it's slightly more.

If you take your $3,000 vacations every year, then every year you're spending $250 per month on your travel. You're already doing this.

That same monthly amount put in the cookie jar will, after a few years, most likely finance the entire points package you need, while you continue to enjoy vacations every year. Simply put, for the same money allocation, you get all three things: the points, a deed of ownership, and great vacations for life, instead of just one trip.

Buying resales...what you don't know can hurt you

Resales aren't always as great a value as they're touted as being. That's not to say one cannot come across a cheap resale timeshare (plenty of them are out there). However, typically it's very wise to do your homework before buying into one.

For the benefit of the reader, I'll note that buying directly from the developer of the resort makes one a first-generation owner. I would consider anything purchased aftermarket to be a resale. With over 30 years of experience working with numerous developers, I routinely run up against the cheap pricing of the secondary resale market. In fact, I hear about resales almost every day. The truth of the matter is, I'm more convinced now than ever that in many cases it's wiser for a consumer to buy directly from the developer over purchasing a resale. Let me explain why.

Although buying direct may initially cost a few dollars more, the developer frontloads the purchase with tremendous value-added benefits lost to a secondary buyer. For example, the developer may prohibit resale buyers from using certain resorts or accessing certain inventory pools in more desirable places. So, although the secondary buyer gets a discount on the points purchase, they don't receive all the benefits, discounts, perks, and value-added options that buyers get when they purchase from the developer.

Certain developers structure their offers this way to protect the original buyers' value and investment. In some cases, in the original transaction, the developer may even secure a right of first refusal or option to buy back. Why would they do that? To control their own resale market later.

Let's say a motivated owner wants to sell at an extremely low price, or even for free. That transaction would have to be pre-approved by the developer. Even with a ready buyer in hand, a developer with a right of first refusal could prevent that sale from happening if the purchase price hurt the overall value of the resort and negatively affected the other owners. The developer may exercise its right to step in and buy at that low price.

The developer, in turn, could put it back on the market with all the original developer benefits and perks at the current market pricing. That's better for the original owner who would have a built-in exit strategy without the hassles of trying to sell later in a resale market. It's a win-win for both the original owner and a new buyer who can deal directly with the developer.

In terms of buying a resale, which would be a second-generation purchase, or a third- or fourth-generation purchase, meaning that it's changed hands, you want to confirm that it's the exact same product you would be getting on a resale market if you were the original owner. I can tell you that most owners have no clue and just say yes to close their sale when, actually, they are unaware that certain benefits may not be available to a resale buyer. *Read the fine print.*

The main reason people purchase in the resale market is the savings. However, hopefully, now you realize that resales can come with hidden and unknown risks that even the original owner doesn't understand.

If you're considering buying a resale, I highly recommend that you ask about the history of the resort and developer. Ask why the seller is getting rid of their ownership. How long have they used it? Have there been any special assessments, or are any forthcoming? For example, after hurricane season in Florida, many timeshare week owners sell their weeks because they don't want to be saddled with a special assessment. An unsuspecting resale buyer wouldn't know that unless they asked. Assessments like these can occur when damage exceeds the insurance coverage or deductible. That's important to know.

On the flip side, points owners may not have any special assessments. There is plenty of insurance coverage and even gap coverage above and beyond the resort's insurance policies. My advice to the consumer is that before they buy a resale, they should ask those tough questions. Otherwise, you could pay a small resale price but encounter big surprises after purchase.

You want to know what benefits are lost or not allowed if you bought the ownership as a resale. These "hidden clauses" do exist. They're out there. Also, remember to ask if current maintenance fees are paid, or would you have to wait another year before using it? What are the closing costs associated with the resale and who pays them? I've seen transactions close on resales in which the new buyer's week was not allowed back into the network. That's another way a developer could govern the resale market.

Typically, with resales, no financing is available and they require a full cash payment. Again, I'm not making an across-the-board ruling for all. However, this book is intended to help you better understand vacation ownership from all sides. Developers usually have easy financing in place, while resale timeshare owners are not in a position to become a bank and must be cashed out. Sellers may even owe money on the original purchase and need to pay it off in full to convey clear title to the new buyer. They're looking to cash out or eliminate any further liability of their maintenance fee or both.

Determining Resale Value

The following factors may influence a timeshare's market value if you are considering a resale.

- » **Ownership type**- Is it deeded ownership or "right to use," a.k.a., term ownership with no deed?
- » **Usage type**- Fixed or floating weeks?
- » **Usage frequency**- Quarter-shares, annuals, every other year, or every third year?
- » **Season-** High-demand, mid-season, or low-demand?
- » **Home Resort-** Location desirability or popularity?
- » **Are they points**- Or weeks ownership?
- » **Evaluation**- What are the points worth in purchase power or evaluation?
- » **Unit Type**-Villa size (studio, one, two, three, four bedrooms)?
- » **Brand**- Major vs. independent?
- » **Exchange affiliation**- Interval International (II), Resorts Condominiums International (RCI), etc.?

Online Timeshare Advertising Agencies

Something else to be aware of are third-party companies that charge unsuspecting owners to list their timeshares. People who must sell or get out of their old timeshare weeks for unforeseen reasons are most vulnerable.

Every now and then, I get calls about those types of solicitations, asking for my opinion as to whether it sounds legit. The call goes something like this.

"Fred, I just got a call from a company that wants to charge me $1,500 but they promised me they'll give me a buyer."

I say, "Stay away!" In my opinion, those are predatory companies. I always want to make sure that people stay away from them, no matter how enticing the offer sounds. Some companies also charge an owner a fee to take over their timeshare. Then they turn around and place the timeshare on the market as an "as-is" resale, offering a buyer a great deal while getting paid twice: once by the seller and again by the new resale buyer.

Not all resale entities are questionable. The more popular resale websites like Redweek.com, eBay.com, and Craigslist list only resale timeshares. They are not brokerages. They do not represent sellers or offer any type of agency relationship for owners who list for sale. Research is left to the buyer.

These are all wise considerations that I hope will help you determine whether it makes sense to buy a resale.

Remember Your Anyway Dollars

To determine whether you are a candidate for vacation ownership, reflect on the way you've been traveling in the past and the typical amount of money you spend. Have you been vacationing once, twice, or more annually? Do you normally spend $200-$300 or more per night on those types of trips? If the answer is yes, you just revealed your anyway dollars because those same exact dollars can be re-purposed to acquire a lifetime vacation ownership package.

To give you an example, I recently sold a vacation ownership package because my prospect was going on a Viking riverboat cruise for a 10-day trip to Europe. He took trips like this each year and routinely spent about $10,000 on similar trips annually because he could afford it and because, in plain English, he was a very fussy guy. He loved higher quality, first-class vacations and was certainly not bashful about letting me know the way in which he traveled.

So, over the past five years, he had spent about $50,000 on trips, and he had no intention of slowing down. I pointed out that his taste in quality trips was well-noted but that he would never get any more value out of those vacation dollars he was currently spending other than *one-time* trips in exchange for a receipt.

We discussed an alternative. I recommended a point package that he could purchase ONCE and that would more than replace the $10,000 per year he was spending...and he could vacation at that level of quality forever. We made his anyway dollars work for him. Wouldn't you like to make your anyway dollars work for you?

Remember Peggy and Her Husband, Henry?

When we last talked about Peggy and Henry, I had gotten to the point in the presentation where we discussed the price. I broke down each trip and came up with the number of points they'd have to purchase to take all the trips Peggy wanted to take. It was at that time when she asked me to step out of the room.

I came back later and, on the table, were their credit card and driver's licenses, which is what I need when a purchase is about to take place. I was astounded! Now, if you know anything about selling, once someone agrees to buy, you don't ask additional questions. You just put down your head and start writing the order.

So, with that, I start drafting the purchase agreement, keeping one eye on Henry. I was concerned he wasn't on board with this decision and would explode at any moment. As it turned out, everything came to a peaceful resolution and all the paperwork was signed, sealed, and delivered within that same visit.

All the tension subsided and was replaced with a sense of calm and acceptance. The atmosphere shifted into happiness and anticipation of exciting times ahead. At that point, it's typically wise to leave things well enough alone, but no, not me...I just couldn't resist the temptation of asking what made them buy.

Fred: "Peg, I've got to ask you one question, please. What in the world made you buy this?"

Without hesitation, she looked at her husband and responded.

Peggy: "He did."

Fred: "Henry made you buy this?"

Peggy: "Yes."

Fred: "I must confess, I'm pretty good at this but I certainly missed it. Can you tell me how that came about?"

Peggy: "Well, I had to talk privately to him, which is why I asked you to leave us alone for a few minutes. I wanted him to know my feelings since he was very clear about his when you put the price up there on the board."

Fred: "What do you mean?"

Peggy: "Well, what did he say when you put the price on the board?"

Fred: "He looked at you and looked at me and said, 'Do you realize it's going to cost about $10,000 a year to go on vacation?'"

Apparently, she took that to mean that he counted himself dead and buried and most likely wouldn't be around for the fourth year.

Peggy: "When we were alone, I looked at my husband and put something into perspective for him. I reminded him that if he was right and we had only three years left after a lifetime together, $30,000 was nothing to me. In fact, no price was too high for me to pay...it would be our last three years! Suddenly it became the most valuable time remaining and priceless to us both. I just wanted him to know that."

WOW! Peg's words hit me like an emotional sledgehammer. How thoughtful. How loving! Even I was reminded of the importance of time over anything else. It became a life lesson and a story I tell others who think that being old means they have to stop living life to the fullest until their last day. Peg minimized the money and placed the importance on *time* in a way I'd never heard in all my years. I became overwhelmed emotionally and even teary-eyed, as did Henry.

Peggy: *(With a chuckle)* "And by the way, Henry, it's obvious we're all going to die but if we're going to go, I prefer we do it together in Paris."

Key Takeaways

Henry and Peggy's story was a tremendous learning experience for me both as a professional in the industry and, more importantly, as a husband and father.

To this day, I share it with others who wish they'd heard of vacation ownership 10 years ago, using this as a lame excuse to do nothing because they're too old. I hope anyone who thinks they are too old to enjoy time well spent, or who is worried to the extent that money rules the choices that really matter, will recognize that much more important things are at risk.

Another reason I like to share this story is that you never know how your decision to vacation or not vacation impacts those closest to you until you sit down and talk about it.

The ultimate question here, as you get closer to your mortality, is: Is "time" worth more or less? Regrettably, many people think time has less value when it's connected to a decision to buy something or incur some financial obligation.

Because of Henry and Peggy's story, I have shifted my focus from selling timeshare to emphasizing the value of shared times.

Here are three important takeaways:

1. Time is filled with either memories or excuses
2. Family feelings matter...so ask!
3. Fun has no age!

Although vacations are personal, if we're being honest, the truth about points is obvious. Vacations aren't free. If your choice to vacation is personally decided with or without points (meaning you're going on your vacations either way), the real choice shifts to how you pay for the vacations you take. With that being clear, consider the following:

You can continue buying vacations using ordinary income or invest a few dollars in a points package and gain the benefits of knowing:

» Points aren't *earned* like income; therefore, they are non-taxable.

» Points are purchased once and are then re-deposited annually...forever.

» Points are willable (deeded).

» Points are inflation-proof currency and will price-freeze future vacations.

Bottom line, points are the better choice.

CHAPTER 6

The Story of Four Buyers

We've talked a lot about Peggy and Henry because they made such a big impact on me. I've dropped pieces of their story here and there throughout the previous chapters, but now I want to bring you in on the full conversation I had with them so that you can get the full picture of why they mean so much to me. Then I'll introduce you to a few other buyers who have their own adventures to share.

Peggy and Henry

Fred: "Peg, you've been married 57 years. I would think you have many vacation memories. Because this meeting is about vacations, how about just telling me about the last three most memorable ones you've had so I can get an idea of what you like to do."

At that precise moment, Henry had reached an early breaking point! There were no answers. No comments. No vacation stories. It was literally 60 seconds of complete, awkward silence. It was deafening and the situation became more uncomfortable by the second, so I broke the silence with what I thought was an ice breaker.

Fred: "Peg, with all due respect, these are the easy questions."

She finally broke out with a snicker and started talking despite Henry's stoic demeanor. I learned that they never took vacations. Regrettably, because of their age, most of their life was now behind them. According to Peg, they didn't do much fun stuff, which seemed to bother her more than it did him. Ironically, I learned, they seemed to have plenty of money when it came to necessities, but spending it on *luxury items* like travel...well, that was another story.

Her husband remained set in his old ways and tried to reel his wife back in check by clapping his hands together and taking control of the conversation. He directed his comments to me.

Henry: "Young man. Do you know how old I am?"

Fred: "No, I'm sorry. I really don't, but you look good."

Henry: "I'm 86 years old. You're asking us about vacations. You're asking us where we would like to go and what we like to do. So, let me be honest with you. I just want to be alive in three years."

Well, that dismal excuse triggered his wife, who apparently had heard it one too many times. Peg took back control of the conversation and suddenly things moved faster and got interesting. In the meantime, her husband became more reclusive, quiet, and madder by the moment. His wife became more engaged, which apparently was not the original plan. You see, before they arrived, they had decided they weren't buying a thing and they'd sealed it with a blood pact. Peg deviated from the plan.

Peggy: "Pick up your pen, young man. I have a few places I'm curious about."

I looked down, picked up my pen, and wrote her requests on the back of the tour sheet as she blurted out destination after destination.

Each time Peg blurted out another trip, she looked over at her husband. There was most definitely an undercurrent between them. She wanted to know more while he wanted to know less.

I wrote one vacation request after another. Peg was on a roll, as well as on what appeared to be a mission. Now, you have to understand what's going on with Henry's disposition. He's getting more aggravated because Peg had become engaged in a full-blown timeshare presentation. After all, that wasn't the plan. She continued her vacation wish list. I took notes and always kept one eye on Henry.

Peggy: "I think we should come back to Florida in the winter when it's cold. For years, we talked about visiting Sonoma in California. We heard that's wine country, right? I know my husband would enjoy that trip because he loves his wine. And what about Italy?"

Peggy had this big wish list that was too good to be true. I could see her excitement, her sparkle, her renewed youth coming alive with all these possibilities. As I said earlier, Peg was 83 years old going on 44 years young, and this proved it. She was totally dialed in, asking the right questions. When we finally visited the villa model, she was blown away, to say the least.

Everything at this point was going well, but Henry...that was a different story. As Peg got more engaged and excited, he got more disengaged. It was a sensitive dynamic, one about which I was becoming nervous because the goal is not to divide and conquer but to create mutual agreement. We were clearly heading in another direction.

If you recall the conclusion of Peg and Henry's story in chapter one, you know that sometimes it takes either a nudge, an epiphany, or a sledgehammer to accept that we go around only once: that a-ha moment when we realize that life is too short to waste on things that don't matter in the end. I recently had another elderly couple in their upper 70s who acted like Peg and Henry, though the situation was the opposite. The wife was totally against spending any money at their age. Her husband, however, just sat back and listened to all her resistance, then looked at his wife and said, "In 25 years, none of the money will matter, will it?"

Heather and Anthony

They're middle-aged, sharp, and have the New York swagger. They have three children and are from Brooklyn. The children were still sleeping so they got their 90-minute tour obligation out of the way while the kids were in the villa.

For the sake of this story, it's imperative that you understand most resort developers give gift premiums, or what I call bribes, to get you to attend these 90-minute presentations. So, most of the time, when guests arrive they make it known that they aren't there to buy anything! Guests are obligated to take the 90-minute tour only if they accept the gift premiums. For the most part, New Yorkers are another story. They come in ready, want what's coming to them, and hold you to the 90 minutes... to the second!

Back to the story. As soon as I walked in to introduce myself, I saw snacks and food scattered all over the small conference table. The resort typically has a snack and beverage area for arriving guests and a private room where we meet and greet them. Apparently, they hadn't had breakfast yet, so they wanted to take advantage of a meal and eat while I talked. After all, no sense in wasting time. There were two bottles of orange juice, two cups of steaming coffee, three blueberry muffins, and two cups of yogurt. Neatly tucked in their beach bag were several bags of chips for the kids.

I fully understand the feeling of needing food. My wife says I get cranky when I'm hungry, and these folks were hungry. No harm done.

Fred: "Good morning, my name is Fred. I see you found the food."

Anthony: "What's up? We were here early and saw the food, so I figured it was okay to grab something."

Fred: "Of course, that's why it's there..."

Heather: "Before we get going, I want you to know that we have three kids sleeping upstairs and we got here 10 minutes ago, so does that come off the 90 minutes?"

Wow, they already had one foot out the door, had gotten a free meal, and were counting down the minutes. This should be fun.

Fred: "Yes, we can deduct the time off your 90 minutes. I'm one of the faster salespeople, so let's get started."

Anthony: "To be very honest with you, we're not here to buy anything."

Heather: "Yeah, I feel bad you got us because I hate to waste your time."

Fred: "Not a problem. You don't have to buy anything, and I don't consider meeting you a waste of time at all."

Anthony: "I just want to be upfront with you. We're here because you called us. You guys offered us a cheap trip to Florida, so I thought, 'What the heck,' but we're not here to buy, just so you know."

Fred: "I got it."

Heather: "Plus, we need to buy a new car as soon as we get home, and James, our oldest son, graduates high school and it's off to college, which we pay for. So, I hope you understand our situation."

Fred: "As I said, you don't have to buy anything, but we do have to be together about 90 minutes, so can I explain how our vacation ownership works?"

Anthony: "Okay, okay, fair enough, but I'm the kind of guy who doesn't need the full sales pitch, so what does it cost?"

Fred: "Why don't we first see if there's even a fit. You told me several times that you're not buying anyway, so let me explain how it works and I'll cover the costs too… I promise."

Anthony: "Fair enough. Let's say I already know how this thing works and I wanted to buy in. What's the bottom line to me?"

Heather to Anthony: "Anthony, we already talked about this in the room. What did you tell me upstairs?"

Fred: "I know exactly what he said. He said, 'No matter what, we're not buying, so don't ask a lot of questions. Just listen and get this over with and we can go to the beach."

Heather: (laughing) "That's funny…were you listening to our conversation?"

Fred: "No, most people feel the same at first. But after I explain everything, they get these a-ha moments, not realizing it was this good of a deal! Then when I get to the money part…

well, that's the best part because we make it affordable and we give you the absolute best deal in the world while you're here on tour! So, if you get enough of those a-ha moments and the deal is right…BUY IT. If not, walk away. Fair enough?"

Anthony: "Sounds good to me. You seem like my kind of guy…no BS!"

Fred: "I was born in New York and raised in the Northeast, so I get it. I know what you want, so I'll cut to the chase and give you guys my very best, bottom-line deal…if you decided you really wanted in."

By this time, I see that the hardcore New Yorkers are becoming more engaged in conversation. We toured the resort and they felt free to express their true feelings about the rooms, the treatment they received while there, and the costs of the program.

Heather: "I have to tell ya, Fred, I love these bigger rooms for the kids because they feel more like apartments. We're not on top of each other. The kitchens are great, too. Does every villa have a kitchen like this?"

Fred: "Yes, they do. And if you're like me, kitchens are the most important room in the house. I love to eat whenever I want. If the food is there, I'll eat it. As far as big rooms are concerned, everybody loves the bigger rooms. What's not to love?"

Anthony: "Let me ask you a question. I heard someone talking by the pool about maintenance fees. I hate paying any kind of maintenance fees every year. Do you guys charge maintenance fees?"

Fred: "As I said, I'll cover all your questions, even maintenance fees, so why don't we finish our tour of the resort first? We'll stop by a media center along the way and wrap up things in my office, where I'll cover all your questions and go over the money part, including how to buy in and become a member."

The 90-minute tour flew by and, in fact, went over time. Heather, who was the most concerned about counting down the minutes, asked the most questions and was very excited about what she learned. The maintenance fee was explained in detail and I was confident that Anthony felt they were easily justified based on everything included!

As I expected, Anthony never stopped negotiating with me, making sure to squeeze every dime he could get. That's a New Yorker for you; they're wired to ask for it all. They buy if they feel they're truly walking away with the very best deal. I believed I had answered all their concerns and I gave them alone time to talk it over between themselves.

I can honestly say to anybody considering buying a timeshare or points package, you will always get your best value there and then! I made sure both Heather and Anthony felt they were getting a fantastic deal loaded with discounts and incentives if they bought that day. At the end of the day, I felt we had made a real connection and I earned their trust and their business.

Northeasterners are the best people to tour simply because you always know where you stand. There's no nonsense or game playing. They are also very loyal if they like you. I will also say that they went on to refer other family members, who later purchased from me as well. Points proved to be a perfect solution at every level. I felt we made a real connection, which is the most important thing because "people do business with people." That doesn't pertain only to New Yorkers, but to all people, and that's the bottom line.

Sarah and Dennis

They were the most polite and courteous couple I'd had in a long time. Timeshare would be great for them. They would appreciate all the benefits and get to enjoy life more than they had been. I learned they hardly ever got away on vacations, which was why they really appreciated this one. I assumed it was long overdue. With that bit of information, I went to work.

After another 60 minutes of explaining the benefits of vacation ownership, touring the resort, and finally answering all their questions, it came down to the final questions, which went something like this.

Fred: "Well, folks, I really would love for you to join our membership, so I have only three questions to ask you. One: Would you like to own something like this for yourself and your family?"

Sarah: "Yes...that would be great!"

Dennis: "I guess I would too if Sarah liked it."

Fred: "Would you use it if you owned it?"

Sarah: "Yes…we would because, you can ask Dennis, we don't waste anything."

Fred: "How about you, Dennis, would you use it?"

Dennis: "Yes, Sarah's right, I don't waste much of anything."

Fred: "Other than the money, is there anything that might prevent you from purchasing today?"

Sarah: "Yes…I'm sorry. We could never buy something like this! Our campground takes all our time and whatever extra money we have."

Dennis: "Yes…we run a summer camp for underprivileged kids, and we're tied up most of the year preparing for that summer season."

Fred: "Wow! That's great. However, I was under the impression that you loved the idea of getting away and that you'd love to do this more often. At least, that's what you told me."

Sarah: "We would but Dennis is so busy repairing the guest cabins. We have 10 of them, you know."

Fred: "I didn't realize you guys ran a camp…that sounds like fun."

Dennis: "It is…but it's a lot of work and it takes whatever money we can muster up. Honestly, it was a bigger project than I figured."

Fred: "How long have you been operating your kids camp?"

Sarah: "It seems like we just got started, but we're going into our 12th year. Dennis's family owned 11 acres that they never did anything with. Dennis and I thought it would make a great kids' campsite and that, through the area churches, we could offer it to kids who never get a chance to camp. We put our idea into motion by working the land ourselves. Dennis built the cabins himself, one at a time. He's handy. We had many people donate items that they weren't using and eventually our campground was ready!"

Fred: "What do you do when you're closed for the season?"

Dennis: "Well, that's when the real work begins. The campground needs constant maintenance and attention from year to year. We have to gather the fallen wood from the winter season and cut it for heating the cabins at night in the fireplaces during the camping season. The plumbing isn't the greatest and I'm always fixing faucets and clogged toilets in the boys' and girls' restrooms. Then there's the repainting, leaky roofs, three bug zappers that need replacing this year, and, of course, our donated golf cart that has a flat tire. The list never ends."

I was blindsided by this and I knew that buying a timeshare would not be that important as a personal retreat for them. Their joy and passion came from helping those underprivileged kids. It wasn't about them at all! It was about others!

At that point, I knew they spent their time and money on their campsite. Their free time went to preparing for the upcoming season. Their reasoning for not taking many personal vacations wasn't typical...it was admirable.

I thought to myself for a moment and started taking the conversation in a completely different direction—helping the kids!

Fred: "Hey guys, let me ask you this. What if the campsite offered something new and exciting for the kids?"

Sarah: "What do you mean?"

Fred: "What if you were to offer the kids an opportunity to win a trip...say, to Disney or a beach resort or rafting down the whitewater rivers in Colorado?"

Dennis: "You mean like a contest?"

Fred: "Yes, something like that. Maybe you have some competitions between the boys' and girls' camps and the winners get a fantastic weekend vacation somewhere!"

Sarah to Dennis: "You know, Dennis, we do have contests throughout the week anyway. Maybe we can offer those same old prizes to the runners-up and one grand prize to the winners at the end of the season before we close the camp!"

Dennis to Sarah: "Didn't you tell me that attendance was kind of dropping off a little and that we had to think of something to bring in more kids? Maybe this would help attract more kids."

Fred: "That's a great idea. I think it would excite the kids to know they could win a trip to Disney or anywhere like that. Imagine the joy of announcing the winning team at the end of the season. Wow! For the losing teams, what if you offered them a chance to pick NEXT YEAR'S WINNING DESTINATION! Those choices of where the grand prize should be from year to year will get them wanting to come back and win. They'll continue to be engaged and excited about coming back for another shot at the grand prize trip!"

All of a sudden I saw them both "light up"! It was as if everything we'd discussed could be used for the kids' benefit! The notion of blessing the kids with not only a camping trip but a chance to win a grand-prize trip...it was the right path and we were back into our discussions of buying a timeshare. The typical buying questions followed. It was a matter of finding an affordable solution, as we'd already discovered the reason *why* they should buy.

Sarah: "What would the least expensive timeshare cost?"

Dennis to Sarah: "Sarah, do you think we can take on another expense with everything I need to tend to?"

Fred: "Let me show you both our smallest package and then we can discuss your options on how to buy it...before anyone jumps to any conclusions. Fair enough?"

Sarah: "Okay, let's see if we can afford this..."

Dennis: "Can you also go over those maintenance fees you mentioned on the cheapest package?"

Fred: "Of course. Let's put our heads together and see if we can make this happen for the kids...they'll be blown away if we can!"

Moral of the story... It's not always about how we personally benefit. Sometimes, purchasing timeshare or points is for the benefit of others. This was such a great experience for us all. Sarah and Dennis went on to purchase and use it year after year, to create memorable experiences for underprivileged children. Their work continues today, and I was honored to be part of their vision and mission. In conclusion, I was touched by their generosity and was reminded of what's important—creating memories and touching lives!

Andrea and Bill

Andrea was a schoolteacher and William (who preferred to be called Bill) was an accountant. I was easily tipped off by their demeanor and preparedness. This was not your typical timeshare tour presentation.

Bill arrived with a folder, pen, and calculator while Andrea brought a list of questions.

The conversation went like this:

Fred: "Good morning. My name is Fred and welcome to our resort. I see you came prepared for something *(jokingly)*. Is this your first presentation?"

Bill: "Oh no, not at all. This is our third time on these timeshare presentations."

Fred: "Wow! Before we get started, can I ask why you didn't purchase during the first two presentations?"

Andrea: "That's easy...we didn't care for our salesperson last year because all he wanted to do was sell us! He immediately started telling us why we should buy in and was pressuring us to decide right there on the spot. I can tell you up front, we're not buying anything today!"

Fred: "Was your last presentation here or at another resort?"

Bill: "Last year we came to this same resort. But as my wife said, we felt pressured and never comfortable because his answers never satisfied our concerns. We didn't click with that guy."

Andrea: "Yes, we came a little more prepared this time and wanted to ask some very pointed questions. Last time all the salesperson did was tell us how good it is to own but he never really answered our questions."

Side note...I was elated to finally have someone volunteer what I normally try to discover. These people had questions! Hallelujah! The fact that they arrived with pen and paper in hand allowed me to zero in on what was most important. In this case, it was *information*. Being sensitive to their desires to learn more, I assured them that this time it would be different. With that, I dove right into their questions instead of doing a canned presentation.

Fred: "Okay, guys, you have the floor. What are your questions?"

Andrea pulled out her list of questions. She wanted me to address her concerns about resort choices, letting their children use their points if they wanted to gift them a vacation, and willing her points over to the children.

I promised I would cover her topics, then turned to Bill for any questions he might have...and why the calculator and folder? This way, I could hear them both out, ensuring that I didn't leave anything unanswered.

Bill's questions were more economic in nature. He wanted to

know specifically what the maintenance fees were and what they included. He also wanted to project those costs with a simple spreadsheet and compare them to his research on inflation. In addition, Bill was concerned about special assessments. He asked if I could tell him how much the maintenance fees had gone up historically, so he could run a scenario over 10 years.

These were very accountant-type questions, and I had to be very direct and complete in my answers. My hands were full. However, I also knew that if I was thorough and not vague, I had a chance to convert them into owners. Before I started, I had a few questions of my own.

Fred: "Hey guys, let me apologize that you never really got your questions answered before. I think they're legitimate questions. But was your reason for not buying because these questions were never addressed, or because you didn't like the answers you got back then?"

Bill: "They were fluffed-over answers as far as I was concerned. Nothing specific, just a lot of double talk by the salesman."

Andrea: "We apologize for venting on you, but we became frustrated with the answers we never got. I honestly felt the prior salesperson was saying anything to make the sale. Sorry, Fred, that you get the brunt of it, but if we're going to buy something that costs this much money, we need complete trust and answers that allow us to decide for ourselves."

Fred: "No need for apologies...but I will ask you this. If I answer your questions completely and to your satisfaction, would you consider moving forward with a purchase? After all, I think that's just as fair a question for me to ask you."

Bill: "Fred, we're here aren't we? We wouldn't come back a third time if we weren't interested."

Fred: "With all due respect, Bill, would you believe that we do get people who have no interest in joining our membership at all but who come for the gift?"

Side note...That was an edgy comment for me to make at that time but because we were being very candid with each other, I had to let them know that not everyone is as forthright as they were. That also whitewashed the possibility of offending them with my direct forwardness as well.

For your benefit, I will list the questions they asked and how I answered them. Before I do, let me make this disclaimer. I'm answering these questions based on my specific company and not all companies. Be advised that not all timeshare organizations or resorts may treat these areas the same way. I strongly suggest that anyone considering a purchase ask these questions because I feel they are important to the buying decision, regardless of what program, membership, timeshare, or points program one is considering.

Thank you, Andrea and Bill, for asking the tough questions for the benefit of our readers.

Andrea's questions:

Q: Will we really get the resort choices we want? We've heard that people have trouble getting what they wanted.

A: Nothing is 100% perfect 100% of the time. Availability is always a factor, even if you buy your reservations with regular money. However, if you want to get what you want 95 out of 100 times, make sure you understand and exercise your membership privileges. Try not to book at the very last second, use your advisor (a real, live person...lol) to book trips, and be open to multiple options, meaning instead of insisting on a three-bedroom villa be open to a two-bedroom plus a one-bedroom villa next door at the same resort. Most people who complain about not getting what they want are facing more of a "user issue, not a system problem." They forget to use their membership's rank and privileges, expect to get high-demand reservations (like spring break or Easter week) at the very last minute, or want to leave within 10 days of booking. In general, those members fail to adhere to best practices in membership advantages and booking.

Q: Can our children use our points if we wanted to give them a vacation instead of going ourselves?

A: Yes, absolutely, and with our membership, there's no charge for that privilege. They simply bring an ID with them after you, as a member, book the trip on their behalf. A good example is, as a wedding gift, booking a fabulous honeymoon for your daughter who just got married.

Q: Are the points willable? How will it work if our children want to get out of it?

A: Yes. The children can be willed the vacation membership points or timeshare week because it comes with a deed of ownership. It's no different from owning a cottage on the lake, which would become part of your estate or your family's assets. The actual *willing* of your vacation ownership deed to the children is something I recommend you discuss with an attorney, but it's done all the time. Your deed is an asset.

Getting out later isn't really a problem either. Divesting follows a pre-determined process that's fairly easy to exercise in our organization. Our company has the right of first refusal to buy it back. You are certainly free to sell it yourself on the open market. There are brokerages out there that specialize in timeshare sales for a commission. As a third option, you can donate it and receive a tax benefit. There are companies that handle that transaction as well. Finally, you can always give it back to the developer, which most likely has the best chance of reselling it because the developer has a sales force and daily prospects on tour every day. For the developer, it's added inventory.

Bill's Questions:

Q: What exactly is included in the maintenance fees?

A: In our organization, as in most, maintenance fees cover all costs to maintain and manage the resort—things like utilities, insurance, labor and staffing, real estate taxes, refurbishing villas, and deferred maintenance. What I mean by that is the big stuff like replacing a roof or repaving a parking lot. Management fees to coordinate all that are also included in one set amount, typically paid annually. It's a turn-key set-up.

Q: Are maintenance fees capped or fixed at a flat amount?

A: No. How can they be if they cover expenses that cannot be capped, as we already discussed? How do you cap real estate taxes? How do you cap utilities? Moreover, if anyone tells you they are capped, you should probably walk away, knowing what you learned. Maintenance fees are expenses that are shared over many members, so they are diluted and therefore easily paid for.

Q: How much have maintenance fees increased in the past?

A: Again, in our case, they have increased 1 to 1.5 cents per point per year and probably will continue along that path. That's an insignificant amount in dollars, especially compared to inflation. The total maintenance fees are divided among the entire membership base, which is increasing and therefore causing dilution. This formula minimizes any spikes or increases in the maintenance fee and spreads any increases among many.

The last thing a developer wants is a high or sudden increase in maintenance fees. That would kill new member sales and make existing members unhappy.

Q: Am I going to get any surprises or special assessments in addition to the maintenance fees?

A: No. Our maintenance fee program is all-inclusive. We are well prepared for the unexpected because we have set up a slush fund within the maintenance fee collected to take care of those occasional unforeseen costs that may otherwise require a special assessment. It's just good money management best practices.

Moral of the story…At the end of our tour, it was clear that Bill and Andrea felt better about their previously unanswered questions. I was sure to ask if I had covered everything. They wrote down every word I said, and Bill was able to calculate a simple projection over 10 years once I gave him the formula. Andrea was relieved to know that the children could take family vacations together in the future and have the means to do so with the deeded points being left in a will.

Bill and Andrea's need for sufficient information before they moved ahead was a learning experience for me. Simply put, some people really need to know the facts. They want answers to the tough questions. They need to write down things and, finally, they need to process that information internally before they act on their decision.

The pressure to make the sale right there, on the spot, may be indicative of the way a pushy salesperson or an aggressive developer wants it done to make budget and produce volume for sales. However, in my opinion, this is a people business and people do business with people. Over the years, I've learned that the way the developer sells the product is not as important to the buyer. Rather, it's the way they, as consumers, buy it. I try to be sensitive to what matters to the individual to whom I'm talking.

Bill and Andrea ended up purchasing from me and I felt great that they were secure in their decision, especially after two failed presentations. So, to all information-driven buyers still seeking answers about vacation ownership, I hope this story helped. Of course, you can always call or email me directly if you aren't getting the tough questions answered. That's yet another reason why I wrote this book.

Why Owners Tend to Buy More

Mrs. Johnson: "Hi, Fred. We're back. I don't know if you remember us, but we just bought from you 11 months ago."

Fred: "Of course, I remember clearly. I appreciate you coming back in. How can I help you?"

Mrs. Johnson: "Can you just go over and explain again what we bought? I'm still confused and have some questions. But to be clear on our end, we're not here to buy anything else. I know we signed up for another sales presentation but we're not buying!"

She said it over and over and over to the point that I told her, "I hear you loud and clear." To further acknowledge her position about not buying that day, I said, "Mrs. Johnson, pretend I have a two-inch paintbrush and dipped it into a can of red paint. Now I'm going to paint a big red 'N' on my chest like Superman's 'S.'

That 'N' in red means I fully understand that you are not going to buy, so please just relax."

Once she felt that she communicated her message to me, she became open to the information she was seeking. Guess what? Ninety minutes later, she asked me if adding more points would allow her to do additional things above and beyond her original purchase about which she was inquiring. She decided to add a few more points despite her initial reluctance. Let's examine why.

You would think the main reason owners buy additional points is to travel more. The truth of the matter is, often it's not about more trips, but rather about higher quality trips. A PointsLife-style is easy to launch with a one-time purchase of points. Adding points later adds currency and enables you to do more. Most of the time, owners really don't know that they want or can do more until I reveal ways to enhance their vacation experiences with a few additional points. It's sort of like "topping the tank." Upgrading should also take into consideration where you are in life in terms of age. People tend to do different things at different times in their lives. It has been said that we go through life in stages.

Our taste for certain things changes as well. When you're younger, affordability is a factor. As you get older, it's about the remaining time you have left to enjoy life. Seniors finally get to enjoy life full-time. Retirement has arrived. Retired folks go from a couple of weeks of vacation during their work lives to having 52 weeks a year with which to create a new lifestyle. The number-one activity for retired people is traveling.

The irony is, older folks tend to be more conservative with their spending. After all, they are living on retirement income and earning less than what they have been earning. I hear this all the time. The truth of the matter is, points spend better than money does. Points are tax-free. Points recycle and renew each year. Points act like a vacation annuity or 401V. Retired folks have worked their entire lives so that retirement will be enjoyable, healthy, and a new beginning. Points are a terrific solution at any age. They simply spend better, spend longer, and spend repeatedly—a means to a much better end. Then you can pass them on to your loved ones. Let's discuss what happens when you no longer need your points.

Some people are not aware that points are willable and can be passed on to loved ones. I call it creating a family legacy. A legacy is the ability to create, or have, an asset that can be willed or passed on. The legal term is to "bequeath" the ownership of this product to other family members down the road. What a great gift to keep a family getting together year after year, even when we go to Heaven, which is my belief.

For my senior-generation vacationers, most of the time it's less about them and more about their children and grandchildren. The notion of leaving behind something of great value is important. Although I will say, not everyone feels this way. I've come across the opposite belief regarding willing ownership to loved ones. I get people who are in their 70s and 80s and who say, "I've done my part; my kids are on their own. Let them fend for themselves." I've learned over the years to be sensitive to other feelings and beliefs and to not make assumptions.

So, why would people upgrade their ownership if they have already bought? Considering what motivates us, different age groups add points for different reasons. Here are a few reasons why owners add more points over time.

Additional points give owners the ability to stay longer on the trips they're already taking. It satisfies that desire of "Oh, just a few more days before we go home, please!" So, instead of a seven-day, why not take a 10-day vacation? Some people can get away only once a year. I say, do it in style, make it a better experience. People add points if they want to upgrade their view or the size of their villa. Maybe they want to go from a one-bedroom to a two-bedroom or from a garden view to an oceanfront. Additional points allow that to happen whenever you want. It gives more quality to what you're doing.

Are you a last-minute or impulse traveler? You may add points to add two- or three-day getaways on the spur of the moment. Those unexpected, spontaneous escapes are what I call "just-because...no reason trips." You wake up and say, "Hey, tomorrow why don't we go away for the weekend?" Sometimes those are the very best vacations, the ones that are unplanned. If that freedom to pick up and get out of Dodge excites you, that would be another reason why you, as an owner, would add points.

Then there are the opposite scenarios. The bigger trips, like Italy or Australia and the like, require more plans and, therefore, more points. With certain points memberships, points can roll over into the upcoming year. Many owners will add points to create a bankable "rollover" that will allow them to take a big trip every other year. Owners can also borrow points from themselves at no charge, making bigger trips possible even with a smaller portfolio of ownership. Europe, here we come!

The reason why owners get to do this is so they can experience higher quality trips at an earlier time in their lives. That's a big advantage to traveling on points as opposed to your hard-earned money. Many consumers may want to go to Europe but refuse to spend the money or simply don't have the money it would take, especially during those earlier times in their lives. You see so many other priorities competing for those dollars that you would love to spend on a European vacation. Points make it possible to do things you ordinarily couldn't or wouldn't do. Points become that fun money or lifestyle money that doesn't interfere with budgetary money.

People add points to gift trips to loved ones.

PointsLife families can do generous things with their points, like providing a fabulous honeymoon to their son or daughter as a wedding gift or a long-weekend resort vacation to a deserving grandchild for graduating from college.

How about a Mother's Day weekend with family to celebrate Mom's special day? Or surprising your wife with beautiful flowers in your hotel room as part of a romantic getaway for Valentine's Day? Husbands out there who are reading this, do you get my point? (No pun intended.) Adding points allows you to add value and quality to the things you love to do.

I had an owner who ended up with an odd number of points he had purchased over the years. He contacted me, asking for suggestions on how he could fairly distribute his points in a will. He had four children and an odd number of points. As opposed to a lopsided distribution amongst siblings, which could turn a nice gesture into ill feelings, I suggested that he simply add a few more points so that it worked out exactly even. He totally agreed, and all four children received the same amount. Problem solved.

Then there are the deal chasers. These are the owners who add points multiple times because they recognize the value, need no convincing, and see what incentives they can get if they buy right there on the spot. I have to say, I love those tours the best...lol. And so, there are many reasons why owners keep adding points to their ownership. Happiness isn't measured in terms of the amount of money you have; it's the people in your life who get to create wonderful memories.

7 Advantages to a PointsLife Style

Advantage #1: Health

There's no question that vacationing has incredible effects in promoting better health. It certainly helps reduce stress. Vacations tend to make you happier...unless, of course, you are planning a trip with a bunch of kids (kidding). Because I have five kids, I feel qualified to say that. Vacations are proven to give you better mental health and clarity. Vacations give your heart a break. I can't think of a better reason to adjust our attitude toward vacationing. We need to include vacations, along with eating right and exercise, in our overall lifetime diet. Getting out of Dodge every now and then makes for a healthy lifestyle with real benefits. Now that you know this...

Live healthy!

Advantage #2: Assurance

Whether you vacation to live out your own passions, travel with your family, or enjoy blessing loved ones who couldn't otherwise vacation, think of the assurance of providing the means (your points) to do so year after year. The enjoyment of living out new experiences, countless adventures, and a world of discovery with them or for them. I call points "the great enabler."

» Points will outlive and outspend your vacation savings.
» Points create a forever commitment to one another.
» Points buy you quality accommodations that are bigger and better for less than the cost of a single hotel room.

Rest assured!

Advantage #3: Family

Family times...reunion times...soul-searching times. Those are invaluable gatherings that bring together everyone as one family. It's those treasured times with your kids. It's opportunities to spoil your grandkids. It's that sheer anticipation of going. In retrospect, we sometimes realize the importance of time too late. It passes by us too fast.

Children become adults in the blink of an eye. A lifetime is a minute. The adage "Take time to smell the roses" is wise advice but rarely taken. The more I work in this industry, the more I'm convinced that "shared time" is a better name than "timeshare." As the father of five great kids, I've learned an important lesson. Shared time makes one's life better. Sometimes the resources, or lack thereof, can get in the way, meaning not everyone has the means to get together even though they may want to.

So, here's some practical advice if you want to see your kids and grandkids more than they can afford. Just pay for everything (lol), and if you are going to pay anyway, use points!

It's a real family advantage!

Advantage #4: Romance

When life's routine and monotony get in the way of fun, it tends to smother the fire and passion for which we all long. Eventually, we can end up in a destination or place we could have avoided—or worse yet, one that we regret. Vacations are ways to create special alone time in exciting places and new environments, forming the oxygen necessary to get those sparks flying again.

A balanced life is a happy life. Maintaining our youthfulness in spirit makes us whole regardless of age. Life should not be about only work, paying bills, and raising a family. It should include time to rekindle our love and passion for one another. It's just as important to live life as an adventure as it is one day at a time.

Take that second honeymoon (or the one you never took). Break away from the kids. It creates that needed time to decompress. If you've finally reached that milestone of being an empty nester, you've arrived at a special time. It's your time. You've earned it. See the world because it's bigger than the one in which you've been living.

Make time to relax and enjoy each other's company as a couple again.

Finally, we've been groomed to live our lives with a plan. However, sometimes having "no plan" is very cool. I've learned that some of the most valuable trips are no-plan, spontaneous, just-because trips. Be romantic!

Advantage #5: Legacy

Life is a gift but celebrating life is a choice. When you decide to make time for loved ones, you add memories, create milestones, and indelibly time-stamp important family events to be talked about forever. Points provide that extra nudge we all need to get off our backsides and do things worth doing.

The legacy passed on is quality time spent with grandparents who can look back and reflect on their lives with a smile. It's generations that get to create family rituals, like a mom, her daughter, and her two granddaughters enjoying a girls' trip to the Big Apple to shop or perhaps to see "The Nutcracker" at Radio City Music Hall. Its Dad, his son, and his grandson sitting in box seats, enjoying that long-awaited Major League Baseball game, which started with a simple game of catch in the backyard.

Legacy moments that we get to do, remember, and reflect on year after year if we're lucky. The gift of remembering vacations we've taken from childhood, where we went, how we laughed and experienced moments that took our breath away.

Create a Legacy.

Advantage #6: In Touch

Each chapter of our lives brings new things and new relationships. Sometimes it's not only the new things that matter but also staying connected with the old. Childhood, high school, and college friends all added relational value to our lives as we reflect on earlier times that meant so much to us.

Sadly, life tends to put distance between friendships, both figuratively and physically. What's so important about the notion of owning points (travel currency) in this context is that it forces us to visit places to which we might otherwise never travel—perhaps revisiting old friends. Think of the joy of attending an annual reunion to relive those special times and laugh like you did when you were a kid.

Or calling your cousin, who was like a brother or sister to you, to reconnect at the upcoming family reunion, knowing you have the resources to stay in the best accommodations. Maybe it's time to revisit your college buddies to see how everyone has aged and how life has been treating them. Imagine leaving behind career obligations, deadlines, alarm clocks, and rush hour for a moment. Wouldn't it be rejuvenating to go on those kinds of relationship trips? I call them "it's been too long" trips—maybe a warm, beachy, tropical rendezvous in Aruba with friends or a weekender in Boston to see the sites, have dinner, and reminisce over good times when life was simple and we were much thinner.

How about getting together and realizing we were all thrilled that we did it? Those goodbyes would certainly be sad but not permanent, as you all agreed to do it again the next year. Friendships bring families together with other families. Vacationing with other families gives us reasons to gather the troops to enjoy those simple things without an iPhone. Old really is new! Playing cards or old-school board games at the dining room table, or roasting marshmallows around a campfire on a chilly night make for good times. You see, life is a gift and time goes by much too quickly to waste it. Make that call...

Stay in touch!

Advantage #7: Impulse

Get away...last-minute decisions work!

It's time you just say "no" and walk away from the demands of more work calling your name. Unwind, if only for a weekend. Take that overdue break or else you might break down. Balance is a choice only you can make. I read an interesting post on Facebook that I feel is worth sharing. It went like this:

"If you were to unexpectedly die, there's a good chance your company would have your replacement hired before the news of your passing hit the obituary." Now that's a scary thought but there may be some truth to it. My mom used to tell me,

"Fred, you take care of *you.*" She was so right because no one else will take care of you...like you.

Key Takeaways

Maybe you're like Peggy and Henry, who never traveled much. However, when you think about the value that travel can add to your relationships, does vacation ownership seem like something worth asking more questions about?

Maybe you're like Heather and Anthony, who are focused on bottom-dollar figures and you're still investigating this concept of a one-time purchase of your future trips.

Maybe you identify more with Sarah and Dennis, who are motivated to find creative ways to use their money to serve others rather than focusing on traveling for personal reasons.

Or are you more like Andrea and William, who are open to the idea but need more answers about the ins and outs of vacation ownership before making a final decision?

Each of these buyers had their own reason for buying and their own processes for reaching that conclusion. As a result, all are now happy owners. It's okay to be a little selfish. It's vital to our overall well-being to take time to recharge, refresh, and replenish ourselves. You can be impulsive. You can also be generous and share your ownership with others without overpaying for the best rooms in the best locations.

Travel
MONDAY
June
27
TUESDAY
June
28
POSTAGE
AIRMAIL
1991
87429
Wanderlust
Packing checklist
water / snack
raincoat

CHAPTER 7

The Buyer's Checklist

What happens during a 90-minute timeshare presentation? Here's a checklist of important things to know and what you can expect if you are intrigued with points and want to see about it for yourself. Most presentations on vacation ownership are about 90 minutes or so, depending on the questions being asked. Some can be much shorter or might run a few minutes longer, depending on your interest level. The presentation should open with a friendly smile and a warm welcome. Next should come an overview to let you know what will be covered. I like to start by making people feel comfortable, reassuring them that this time together will be worthwhile and resourceful for them; it will be nothing more than an open and friendly conversation to get all their questions answered. It's their time, so we spend it wisely on things important to them. No canned pitches with me! Every meeting is customized to the prospective clients' questions and concerns.

Next, I give you a tour of the resort and take you through one of our villas so you can get an idea of the quality, decorating styles, and great views you can get with a membership. Then our state-of-the-art media center will take you on a whirlwind tour around the world in 3-D, so you can see incredible places and destinations, as well as the variety of things you can do.

Finally, we'll end up in my office, where I'll go over the economics, costs, and numbers. I'll typically ask about your travel preferences, so I can help point out the ownership features you may like most. Of course, I welcome questions. For me, your questions are good because they allow me to zero in on what's important to you.

So, that's what happens during a 90-minute presentation, at least one with me.

Are You Objective?

My advice is to come with the attitude that it's okay to NOT buy, but it's NOT okay to not learn, because you might learn something you didn't know—those a-ha moments that I alluded to in earlier chapters, during which you get revelations about faulty preconceived notions stemming from myths and prior experiences. Perhaps, before meeting me, you participated in a timeshare presentation that was not enjoyable. It might have been high-pressure, it might have been something less than what you had hoped for, or the product may have made little sense. This makes it hard to be open-minded when you attend another 90-minute points presentation that offers a quality product and that is hosted by a friendly, well-spoken, and informative professional. If I can give you some advice, even if we never meet, it's to avoid carrying old-school timeshare baggage into a points presentation because...it's not what you think.

The Buyer's Checklist Continued...

The best questions to ask depend on what's important to you. The list below features generic questions that I think anybody would want to have answered in a manner that helps the prospective client understand exactly what the sales representative is offering. The tour is all about making sure your questions get answered, so I encourage you to dig in and ask as many of the questions below as you want. If you need more details, add follow-up questions.

Not everything in this list is applicable to every transaction, but I want it to apply to a variety of situations.

1. How does it work? Suppose I'm a member; walk me through the process of using points.

This question is in the spirit of being coachable and ready to learn something. Ask them to describe the actual process. Does a part of the process seem difficult? Do they have tips on how to make it easier for you?

Wouldn't you want to know something like that?

2. What am I buying?

Do I get a deed? Is my ownership limited to a certain timeframe? Is it limited to a certain-size villa? A certain view? How much vacation time do points really give me?

Ask for specifics beyond the generic sales rhetoric. I think those are all fair questions because they give you a basis for comparison and help clarify what you're buying.

There are different types of vacation products that one could buy. A "right-to-use" does not come with a deed of ownership. In my opinion, that's a substandard vacation ownership product because, as a real estate broker for 34 years, I'm an advocate of owning something instead of renting it, if the money is about the same. It makes ownership better over time. That's good old-fashioned advice from over three decades of real estate experience.

3. I have children. Is this something I can put in a will?

If you get a deed with your ownership, you should be able to include it in your estate and pass it along to family in a will. However, it won't hurt to ask for clarification.

4. What happens if I don't want it anymore...what then?

I'd love for you to buy points and use them forever and ever. However, everyone is different and so is every situation. So, it's wise to understand what happens should you ever decide to sell.

Here are more questions that dig deeper into exit strategy options:

» **What is the developer's position on resales? Does the developer have a buyback or surrender program that gives me comfort if I or my children no longer want it?**

» **What is a resale and why wouldn't I just want to buy a resale?** I know we talked about this in an earlier chapter, but wouldn't this make for an interesting conversation? Hear out these answers.

5. Can I let my children or someone else use my points? If so, are there additional fees?

That's a common question I get. For us, it's a simple process with no extra fees, but you'll want to know how it works with your resort or developer.

6. Can I split up the time to use less than a week or maybe more than a week? Are there fees for breaking up the time?

This may seem like an odd question given how much we've discussed the flexibility of points, but it's in your best interest to get an answer to this question while you're sitting with your sales rep. If you buy something that's a seven-day-week timeshare product and you want to use it for three days, are fees associated with that?

7. How many existing members are there?

You'll want to know how many existing members there are because that will directly impact your ability to get what you want when you want it. See, the greatest strength of timeshare or vacation ownership is also its greatest weakness.

The greatest strength is that your reservations come out of members-only protected inventory so that you're assured of getting what you want when you want it. However, its greatest weakness is that the inventory is allocated for members, so you need to know how they're balancing the number of members and what's available. This is a great question to ask.

In two words: "Explain reservations."

8. What are maintenance fees? Do you have them? What do they include?

Maintenance fees are a necessary feature and benefit that is often the most misunderstood topic. They ensure a turnkey, hassle-free membership experience for owners/members. They should include real estate taxes, management fees, utilities, all insurances, staffing, labor to run the resorts, and a budget for refurbishing units on a regular basis.

The litmus test of how well the company is managing with maintenance fees is to look around the location where you are staying. Look at the condition of the resort and see if what you're about to pay for is providing what they're proclaiming.

If they say the maintenance fee will do all this stuff but you look around and see beat-up, shabby, dated, and dull facilities, I would take that as an indication that this may not be for me. By the same token, if the resort looks great, crisp, new, and modern, and if people are walking around with smiles, that's an indication that the company is on its game. That would be a big plus for me, and hopefully for you as well.

9. How much have the maintenance fees increased in the past five years?

A fair question to ask is "Let's go back five to 10 years. Have your maintenance fees gone up and, if so, by how much?" Most likely, the sales rep is motivated to sell you something, which is understandable. My motive for this book is to provide you with good insight so you can make informed choices.

Now, I will temper this by saying that you shouldn't be afraid of a maintenance fee, as we've covered how a maintenance fee is part of owning anything. You just want to make sure it's a good program.

Here's the "buyer beware" warning. Beware of anybody who says their maintenance fees are fixed or flat and that the fees will never increase. That's like a car salesman telling you, "If you buy the car now, I guarantee gas will never go up more than $2." If you hear that, get up and walk away. No one can predict what real estate taxes, insurance policies, utilities, or labor costs will be tomorrow, so there's no way to fix a maintenance fee that covers them.

The objective of a maintenance fee is not to create a bill for you. It's to create an enjoyable environment for you. However, you want to make sure it doesn't get crazy. You're asking for a history of it because if the maintenance fees escalate excessively over a short period of time, that's an indication that some mismanagement might be going on.

10. Is financing available? What are the terms? Is there a pre-payment fee? What is the length of the term?

"Is there financing?" is obviously a great question. Even if you're considering paying in cash, you'll want to understand what the financing terms would be should you opt to go with the company's financing program and keep your money in the bank.

11. Are there membership dues?

If there are separate membership dues, what is their purpose? What support can you expect for paying them?

Here are some examples of what maintenance membership dues might include:

A. Collaterals Kit/Membership Kit. These are the hard goods you walk out with. The kit might have DVDs, CDs, resort directories, and all kinds of things that provide instant information about what your membership includes.

B. Online Membership Account. Your fee may include an online account so that your points can be redeposited annually into your account, like an online checking account. You want to know that you have direct access to that account if it's a points-based system so you can track how much you've spent and when new deposits are made. Usually, it's an online portal.

C. Your Travel Membership Website. This is typically the central nervous system of your entire membership. It's your online back office where you can research, access, and book trips. It's a place, phone number, or both that enables you to access information. See and compare the variety of options. Learn about unique destinations and maybe see the rooms via pictures before you book. Look up critical information like how far the resort is from a nearby hospital or airport. The website should show you things like that. Does the resort have onsite restaurants? Are there actual pictures of the accommodations that you can review so that, upon arrival, you're not underwhelmed but rather are overwhelmed and happy?

D. An Advisor. The better vacation ownership organizations will typically provide this support. The superior ones will even provide you with a customer rep or an advisor who can book trips for you personally. It's like a personal concierge, a personal travel agent, or a personal travel advisor. Your membership fee typically includes all this.

Some Other Questions to Ask:

» When can I book my first trip?
» Can I bring my friends, family, or dog?
» Are there any tutorials, directories, or books to guide me through the booking process?
» Is there somebody who will help me? Whom do I talk to if I have questions?

Making the Buying Decision

After you get all the answers to your buyer list questions, it's time to ask yourself three key questions:

1. Would I like to own something like this for myself and my family?
2. If I own this, would I use it?
3. Is there anything, other than the price point, that would prevent me from moving forward with this?

I think everybody should have recreation or leisure in their life so that they can step back and not always work. For some people, it's a swimming pool. For others, it's a lakeside cabin or cottage. For many of today's vacationers, freedom and flexibility rule the day. It's a PointsLife product. My goal is to make sure that important piece exists in your life. Taking time to recharge, reconnect, or relax is often held hostage to what's available in your checkbook.

If you make yours a PointsLife, you will be forced to go more, which is the part I like best.

People come into most 90-minute presentations with a blood pact to not buy anything regardless of how good it sounds. If you have read my book, I don't believe this is necessary for you. Your buying decision should be based on what is best for you.

The worst thing that could happen is that you don't buy anything, while the best thing that could happen is that you walk out with something that can make you happy for years to come. Your salesperson's goal is the latter, to make you happy.

Remember, no one can sell you anything against your will. After all is said and done, you decide if you want to own it.

Also, remember that vacation ownership is not an experiment. It has been around for over 60 years and has evolved into a highly efficient currency-based system that's right for the times. It works for hundreds of thousands of owners today and it just might work for you.

Key Takeaways

All timeshare companies and salespeople don't do exactly what I would do during a 90-minute presentation, but they'll follow a similar pattern. My goal is to prepare you for what happens during a presentation tour, so you'll feel more at ease before you sit down at the table. Neither one of us knows whom you may be sitting in front of, but these questions should get you all the information you need to make an educated choice.

Even if you get the right questions answered and even if those answers satisfy you, you might still be reluctant to move forward. That's human nature. Nobody wakes up in the morning deciding to purchase timeshare during a sales tour. You're always going to wonder, *Am I doing the right thing?* It's a normal thought process, and that's okay.

If you feel that the questions were answered to your satisfaction, it makes sense, it's affordable, and you would go on vacations either way, BUY IT. Buy it and enjoy it. Keep your vacation planner handy and revise it when necessary to help optimize your points.

A Special Message of Thanks from Fred

A message to the timeshare sales professionals in our industry. If you are reading this book, I want to say thank you. Thank you for caring about what our customers are looking for and putting their needs ahead of ours. Thank you for being sensitive to their fears and to the prior experiences that may have prevented them from learning more. I am thoroughly convinced that if we better understand our customer, we become better servants. We still have much to learn regarding our profession, but we have made much progress.

A message to our valued customers of tomorrow. If you were on the fence or apprehensive about vacation ownership, I hope this book helped you better understand the possibilities. I want to say thank you. I am confident that if you apply the principles and ask the right questions, you will get the answers you are seeking. If you have never been on a 90-minute presentation tour with me, consider this our introduction to each other. Please regard me as a resource for you. I would also love to hear from you, so feel free to join my user group on Facebook at PointsLife. In addition, you can message me should you have questions or want to visit my resort in Florida.

In closing, thank you for considering making your life an adventure, a discovery, and a blessing to others around you.

Thank you for making your life…a PointsLife.

ABOUT THE AUTHOR

FRED LANOSA, author, speaker, and coach, is no newcomer to success. His career spans over 30 years, and he has helped thousands of families in vacation timeshare and real estate. His journey has provided invaluable insights into how consumers perceive—and often misunderstand—vacation ownership. Those insights created the need for this book. Fred is still active today as a recognized, respected, and recommended sales professional at the cutting edge of where the vacation ownership industry is headed. His lifetime commitment to continual learning and coaching others has won him national leadership awards not ONCE but from five major-brand organizations. Through those experiences, Fred recognized another passion: mentoring others as a speaker/trainer and coach traveling the national speakers' circuit throughout North America. In 2012, he joined Marriott Vacation Club as a sales executive on "the mainline" and within six months had become Rookie of the Year. He went on to earn numerous top sales achievement awards and was nominated by his

peers to receive the 2015 and 2018 Marriott Award of Excellence. Fred has transcribed this astounding journey into a powerful, easy-to-read book designed as a resource for today's consumer looking to better understand vacation ownership. His website is www.fredlanosa.com.

A SPECIAL VACATION OFFER FROM FRED

★★★

Experience a 3-Day PointsLife Vacation For Yourself

You're invited to spend three sun-drenched days as my guest on one of Florida's most beautiful tropical paradise islands. While there, you'll attend my 90-minute informational seminar that covers everything you need to know about "Points". The rest of the time, you're free to stick your toes in the sand, immerse yourself in blue ocean waters, and experience a PointsLife vacation for yourself. It's easy. Just contact my reservations department below to reserve a 1-bedroom or a 2-bedroom villa at a special low package rate. You can also bring along family and friends to see it for themselves at no charge. You'll be staying at our world-class oceanfront resort. To reserve your PointsLife vacation package, just contact us. Once you secure a spot, you'll have up to 12 months to book your trip and use it. Questions? Feel free to email me personally at Fred@ThePointsLife.com or go to www.fredlanosa.com for trip details.

I look forward to meeting you personally.

Author, Coach, Speaker

Recognized...Respected...Recommended

44526619R00089

Made in the USA
San Bernardino, CA
19 July 2019